DEMOCRACY HAS ROOTS

E
183
658

DEMOCRACY HAS ROOTS

M. L. WILSON
Under Secretary of Agriculture

PREFACE BY

CHARLES A. BEARD

CARRICK & EVANS · INC ·
NEW YORK

COPYRIGHT, 1939, BY CARRICK & EVANS, INC.

A

PRINTED IN THE UNITED STATES OF AMERICA

TO THOSE
WHOSE FAITH IN DEMOCRACY
CALLS FORTH NEW METHODS
TO MAKE IT WORK

6476

CONTENTS

THE significance of this volume outruns the mere matters of fact and questions of technical administration mentioned in its pages. In purpose and conception it encompasses American life and reflects the spirit of American government. Hence it is directed to those who live in cities as well as to farmers on the land.

There was a time, not many years ago, when writers on economics and public policies seemed to imagine that the United States was destined to follow the lines of British development, that manufacturing industry would continue to expand, while agriculture would be reduced to a smaller and smaller role in the affairs of the country. Books on industrial economy multiplied, outstripping in number and weight of thought treatises on land economy. For a brief time after the World War, experience seemed to confirm the prophecy. An upward swing in American loans abroad was followed by an increased export of manufactured goods. The proportion of agricultural produce in the total export kept on its downward trend. Thus decided countenance was given to the old idea that agriculture was destined to drop in pecuniary and cultural importance and that urban industry was bound to rise indefinitely, if not forever.

Now the outlook for ever-expanding outlets abroad to absorb the ever-expanding potentials of manufacturing industry is clouded and the idea of endless urbanization fades. The very course of events has forced a reconsideration of the place of agriculture in the United States—as a way of life, as a source of enlarged buying power, and as a cornerstone of democratic liberties. With growing insistence the thought of industrialists and statesmen is directed to the new turn in American affairs. The Federal Government, which for generations has favored manufacturing and shipping by tariffs, subsidies, bounties and technical assistance, now grapples with the problem of an economic balance, seriously and tenaciously. And as foreign economies are being transformed, it is likely that the landward trend in American thought and practice will take on increasingly the character of an unavoidable necessity.

It is against the large background thus inadequately sketched that the pages which follow assume fundamental significance for the whole country. The lectures on which they are based were delivered in the Department of Agriculture. The choice of themes was determined in the Department. The upshot in general represents the broad outlook of the Department. It is true that none of the chapters, nor the book itself, is "official," in the sense that it exactly expresses departmental views. But the volume is evidence that the Department as now administered has passed far beyond mere interest in the technics of agriculture and is deeply concerned with the relation of that branch of economy to American life in its widest ranges. It is a contribution to a growing unity of thought about American affairs—a needed offset to the former overemphasis on the role and future of manufacturing enterprise alone.

A second striking feature of the volume before us pertains to the subject of public administration, so often regarded as lifeless, bound by red tape, and devoid of spirit. Participants in every large undertaking carried on by a hierarchy of power tend, if left to the natural course, to routineering, to absorption in the immediate task, and to indifference in respect of larger objectives. The new science of administration, public and private, has taken cognizance of this bureaucratic tendency and seeks to overcome it in each large-scale enterprise by drawing officials and employees into the large councils of the undertaking, by giving them insight into its broad purposes, and by laying stress upon the related nature of all specific operations.

Upon this subject of efficient administration

in a democratic society the volume before us has a distinct bearing. The conception and execution of the work show that the Department of Agriculture, in organizing and carrying on its prescribed duties, is striving to draw its officials and employees into "the large councils," to stimulate their interest in the processes of American democracy, and to indicate the relations of detailed performances to the needs and spirit of American society. As a matter of fact about a thousand members of the Department attended the lectures and about seventy-five of the principal administrative and policy-forming officers took part in the smaller conferences which followed the formal discourses. In the give-and-take of the experiment the barriers of official gradations were broken down, as officials, employees and lecturers concentrated their attention upon the broader aspects of the detailed work in agricultural administration.

Beyond the confines of the Department news of the experiment spread, as reports of the transactions appeared in the press. Members of the Department employed in the field, workers in the Extension Service, instructors in Agricultural Colleges and farmers wrote to the Department asking for fuller accounts of the lectures and discussions. In response to these inquiries, M. L. Wilson, Under Secretary of the Department,

aided by Mrs. Helen Hill Miller, condensed and
edited the proceedings, for the purpose of making
the substance and essence of the discussions available to the wider public. Surely it is a sign of a
better day in administration when such an undertaking can be carried out by a Department of
Government voluntarily with a view to invigorat-
ing its own work and informing the public.

Although my part in the departmental experiment was small—limited to a single lecture and
participation in one discussion, it so happens that,
as a dairy farmer, I have had numerous and inti-
mate contacts with officials and employees of the
Department both in Washington and in rural regions. I have carried local issues up to Washington for consideration and action. I have seen
agents of the Department in fields and barns and
farmers' meetings. I have watched them make
studies of soils, of erosion, of conservation problems. With my neighbors in Connecticut I have
sat down in conferences with representatives of the
Department to debate, thresh out and settle complicated and vexatious issues of marketing, production allotments and land uses. And I can bear
witness to the fact that the representatives of the
Department with whom I have come in contact
in offices, farmers' meetings, on the land and in
forests have the capacity to make clear the work
they are engaged in, to give the reasons for it, and

are fair-minded and exacting in requiring compliance with law and rule.

Space does not permit, nor does command of language allow me, to give a living picture of the ramifications of this vast national agency and its contacts with life on farms—from the hills of Connecticut, where I make my home, to the cotton fields of South Carolina, where this prefatory note happens to be written. Yet out of my own observation I can say truly that nowhere in its work have I seen a spirit of bureaucratic regimentation made manifest in word or deed. Social order itself requires laws and rules, but in a democratic society these commands are expressions of popular opinions matured into decisions and accepted in the light of such reason as we can command. The Department of Agriculture operates in this spirit. The pages that follow reflect it.

CHARLES A. BEARD.

Columbia, South Carolina,
January, 1939.

THE well-functioning of the democratic process, now and in the years to come, is a matter
which American citizens across the entire country,
both in cities and on farms, hold to be of first
importance. Thousands of American men and
women are convinced that so far as the United
States is concerned, democracy has roots that
penetrate deeply and enduringly into the social
structure. At the same time, they believe that the
developing institutions which over a century and
a half have served the sound purposes of the republic are the product neither of inflexible deter-
minism nor of blind chance. They believe that
the vitality of the American democracy of today
stems from the creative care given by successive
generations of practicing democrats to the seed-
ling planted by the founding fathers. And they
believe that the work of past generations has laid
an obligation on those now living.

This book, which examines some of the quali-
ties of the soil required for democracy to flourish,
is offered as a contribution toward that obligation. It contains a summarized version of the
facts and points of view presented in some lec-

tures and informal conferences on the democratic
process held by the Department of Agriculture in
the first half of 1938, and participated in by a
group of men and women outstanding in various
fields of the national life, and by a large part of
the Department of Agriculture staff.

The series of lectures, given under the auspices
of Dean A. F. Woods of the Graduate School of
the Department of Agriculture, included examination of both the setting in which American
democracy operates and the techniques through
which it is currently expressed. Charles A. Beard,
as dean of American historians, was asked to orient the group for its survey of the domestic background of democracy. Certain of the non-rational
factors, the traditions, the folklore, which have
played a part in the rise of American civilization,
were expanded by a lawyer, Thurman Arnold,
and an anthropologist, Ruth Benedict. Following
their discussion of non-rational forces, Paul B.
Sears examined the rational approach to modern
problems attempted by the various sciences.

But the domestic scene is only part of the setting of American democracy. The United States
is part of a world in which the nation as expressed through Communism, Fascism and National Socialism is competing with the nation as
organized democratically. The objectives and
accomplishments of the chief competitors of

democracy were analyzed by Arnold Wolfers, and problems relating to the making of American foreign policy were considered by Raymond Leslie Buell.

Following this survey of the general setting of American democracy at home and abroad, attention turned to specific devices for political action. James K. Pollock examined the place of the political machine and George H. Gallup described his experience in polling public opinion.

Next, a more inclusive analysis of the general operations of the representative system in the United States was given by Sir Willmott Lewis; Secretary Henry A. Wallace then explored the sources of authority and discipline in American democracy.

The importance of local initiative in policy-making was emphasized by Francis Pickens Miller; Bruce Bliven described the prerequisites to a proper functioning of the press.

In the field of national government, T. V. Smith spoke on the legislative branch, and Walton H. Hamilton on the judiciary in a changing world; Herman Finer's consideration of the proper conduct of administrative organs touched directly on the immediate problems of the Department of Agriculture.

The basic materials for this book were thus provided by the distinguished men and women

who were willing to come, often at considerable
sacrifice of time and energy, to discuss democracy
with the Department of Agriculture staff. Further
contributions were made in the course of the
informal conferences which followed each lecture,
and at one or another of these discussions the staff
had the benefit of brief remarks by an additional
group of collaborators to whom recognition is
also due: R. N. Benjamin; Benjamin Brown;
Turner Catledge; Raymond Clapper; F. R. Moul-
ton; George W. Norris; John H. Provinse; C. E.
Robinson; Ralph E. Turner; W. W. Waymack;
James Russell Wiggins; Josephine Wilkins.

The editing which has been undertaken has
been done in order to bring the material within
convenient compass, to combine what was said
informally with what was presented in lecture
form, and to point up its pertinence to American
agriculture in the democracy of today. In order
to accomplish this, a certain amount of rearrange-
ment and regrouping has been done. Comments
made and points of view set forth at the staff
conferences have been interwoven with the remarks of the lecturers. The lecture material in
the first chapter, "Early Democracy and Early
Agriculture," is chiefly that presented by Dr.
Beard. Chapter II, "Applied Science and Applied Folkways," is derived from Dr. Sears, Dr.
Benedict, Dr. Arnold and Dr. Smith. Dr. Wolfers

and Dr. Buell are the chief contributors to Chapter III, "The Way of Dictatorship"; Chapter IV, "The Way of Democracy," is drawn from Secretary Wallace, Sir Willmott Lewis and Mr. Miller. "Instruments of Policy-Making" described in Chapter V include those discussed by Mr. Bliven, Dr. Pollock, Dr. Gallup and Dr. Smith. Dr. Hamilton and Dr. Finer provided the lecture material in Chapter VI on "Judges, Experts and Administrators"; the final chapter, "Contemporary Democracy and Contemporary Agriculture," is drawn from the remarks of Dr. Finer, Dr. Sears and the editor.

Special mention should be made of the work of Mrs. Helen Hill Miller who, under the chairmanship of the editor, acted as secretary to the Committee which arranged for the discussions on democracy and assembled the material here presented.

Probably none of the many participants in this venture in democracy would agree with all the statements contained in the following pages; certainly the editor does not. Complete agreement would probably be confined to one principle: that the different views on these vital questions held by responsible citizens should have the widest possible hearing.

M. L. WILSON.

CHAPTER I

EARLY DEMOCRACY AND EARLY AGRICULTURE

AT THE time of the establishment of the Federal Union, about ninety-five out of every hundred Americans were engaged in agriculture, and Jefferson wrote:

"I think our governments will remain virtuous for many centuries; as long as they are chiefly agricultural; and this will be as long as there shall be vacant lands in any part of America. When they get piled upon one another in large cities, as in Europe, they will become corrupt as in Europe."

A generation and a half later, out of every hundred people counted, the country had lost nearly two to the city, but America was still ninety-three percent agricultural. Webster wrote:

"Of our system of government the first thing to be said is, that it is really and practically a free system. It originates entirely with the people and rests on no other foundation than their assent. To judge of its actual operation, it is not enough to look merely at the form of its construction. The practical character of government depends often on a variety of considerations, besides the abstract frame of its constitu-

tional organization. Among these are the condition
and tenure of property. . . . The history of other
nations may teach us how favorable to public liberty
are the division of the soil into small freeholds and
a system of laws, of which the tendency is, without
violence or injustice, to produce and preserve a degree of equality of property. . . . With property divided as we have it, no other government than that
of a republic could be maintained, even were we
foolish enough to desire it. There is a reason, therefore, to expect a long continuation of our system."

On their fifth round, the census takers recorded
another agricultural loss that was a city gain; the
United States was now 91.6 percent agricultural.
From the vantage point of his old age, Madison
looked ahead a hundred years toward the nation
of 1929:

"The United States have a precious advantage also
in the actual distribution of property, particularly
the landed property, and in the universal hope of
acquiring property. The latter peculiarity is among
the happiest contrasts in their situation to that of
the Old World, where no anticipated change in this
respect can generally inspire a like sympathy with the
rights of property. There may be at present a majority of the nation who are even freeholders, or the
heirs and aspirants to freeholds; and the day may not
be very near when such will cease to make up a
majority of the community. But they cannot always

so continue. With every admissible subdivision of the arable, a populousness not greater than that of England or France will reduce the holders to a minority. And whenever the majority shall be without landed or other equivalent property, and without the means or hope of acquiring it, what is to secure the rights of property against the danger of an equality and universality of suffrage, vesting complete power over property in hands without a share in it; not to speak of danger in the meantime from a dependence of an increasing number on the wealth of a few? In other countries, this dependence results in some from the relations between landlords and tenants; in others, both from that source and from the relations between wealthy capitalists and indigent labourers. In the United States the occurrence must happen from the last source; from the connection between the great capitalists in manufactures and commerce and the numbers employed by them. Nor will accumulations of capital for a certain time be precluded by our laws of descent and distribution; such being the enterprise inspired by free institutions, that great wealth in the hands of individuals and associations may not be unfrequent. But it may be observed, that the opportunities may be diminished and the permanency defeated by the equalizing tendency of the laws."

Four contemporary documents concerning that nation of 1929 toward which Madison was looking substantiate much of his prophecy. Berle and

Means' "Modern Corporation and the Idea of
Property" shows the intervening concentration of
economic power. A comparable concentration of
wealth as registered by the distribution of income
is shown by the work of the Brookings Institution
on "Income and Economic Progress" and "America's Capacity to Consume," and by the National
Resources Committee's study of "Consumer In-
comes in the United States." And the Report of
the President's Committee on Farm Tenancy
shows a parallel decline in individual farm ownership from 74.4 percent of all farmers in 1880
to 57.9 percent in 1935.

By the beginning of the 1930's, moreover, agriculture's majority in the nation had dwindled to
a minority. The census of 1930 showed 56.2 percent of the population to be urban and industrial,
and Jefferson's statement—

"But the great mass of our people are agricultural;
and the commercial cities, though, by command of
the newspapers, they make a great deal of noise, have
little effect in the direction of the government"—

is no description of the America of today.

The shift in the balance of power from country
to city was closely related to the limits of exploit-
able resources. Pre-emption of the natural resources in which the farmer was interested ended
with the occupation of the last of the fertile land.

Thereafter the economic base of the agricultural segment of the American community was land already in use. Ill-used, it was subject to rapid deterioration, as attested by the record scrawled in a million gullies across its surface. Well-used, its productivity could be increased, by taking advantage of the new technology—by improved plant and animal strains, by mechanized cultivation, by chemical fertilizers, sprays, treatments. But the amount of possible improvement was limited, and the economic advantage obtainable from it was still further restricted by the highly competitive position of the individual farm.

The conversion of other continental resources into private property was not subject to comparable limitations. The progress of invention kept open the frontiers of new enterprise. Unlike crops, products like coal, ore, oil, were not subject to the slow cycle of the zodiac; they were much more easily tied to the rapid turnover of Fortune's wheel. The resulting magnetism of the economics of iron, steel and electricity as contrasted with the economics of agriculture is demonstrated by any map that shows concentrations of population in the United States today.

But in one respect the closing of the physical frontier affected the rest of the nation as much as it affected the farmers. The closing of the frontier unified American life and compelled succeeding

generations to live with the past and with each
other. The United States was then added to
the list of what Madison called "countries fully
peopled," and was forced to begin to meet problems whose solution the existence of the frontier
had long deferred.

Since the closing of the frontier, the problems
of the United States have shown many characteristics in common with the problems of the older
nations of the Western world. Yet each type of
civilization has its own style and characteristics
and the tradition which Americans bring to the
solution of their problems differs in some notable
respects from the traditions of the countries from
which the early American settlers came.

In the first place, the United States has never
had an established church in the European sense,
that is to say, a church whose hierarchy rested
upon the possession of great estates in land which
rendered it economically independent of the rest
of society. It is true that in some of the colonies
the church of England was by law the established
church, but in no colony on the eve of the Revolution was conformity to that church enforced by
law. Affirmation of religious liberty was a typical
article of the various Revolutionary Bills of
Rights, and voluntary contribution has since been
the normal source of church support.

The characteristic church structure of the

founding period, particularly in New England, was the congregation. The first New England settlements were made by men and women of a common congregation, and the relation between democracy and the independent congregation has been close throughout western civilization. The congregation was no less important in the period of continental development. During the westward advance whole congregations simply migrated from the old settlements to the frontier. As a result, American religious life, particularly in those aspects of the church that relate to power, has been different from that of Europe.

In the second place, there has been no feudal aristocracy in America. It is true that there were great landlords in the Hudson River Valley, manors in Maryland, and plantations in the South, where the land was entailed by the law of primogeniture according to the feudal rule. But while these estates had aristocratic features they were not comparable to the landed estates in Europe; the so-called landed aristocracy of America had no prestige, no special legal position, special privileges of government that set it off from the rest of society as the aristocracy of Germany and France and England was set off from the rest of society.

In the third place, American civilization, unlike that of Europe, has never included a military

caste. In England, France and Germany the officers of the army were mainly recruited from the
landed gentry; in Germany that is still true today.
A citizen army as contrasted with a standing army
was from the first characteristic of both the philosophy and the practice of the American people—
the farmer with his rifle over the mantelpiece was
the reality to which constitutional dignity was
given in the declaration that the right of the people to bear arms shall not be abridged.

Nor, in the fourth place, has America had a
bureaucracy in the European sense of the word, a
hierarchy of officers separated from the rest of
society, people with a special prestige, a special
sense of being the permanent repository of the life
of the state. The bureaucracy of Louis XIV sur-
vived the French Revolution to be restored by
Napoleon and remain down to the present as a
powerful hierarchic force in the French Republic;
but the American Revolution made a clean sweep
of the former English official bureaucracy, and
the officeholders of succeeding decades were far
from being a permanent group.

The absence of these four hierarchies, ecclesi-
astics, landowners, military men, and permanent
public officials, has caused the exercise of power
in the United States to assume patterns different
from the patterns of the older countries of the
Western world, even when dealing with the eco-

nomic and social changes which in the course of recent years have been common to all alike.

For these reasons, to an extent unparalleled elsewhere, patterns of power in the United States have been undisguisedly economic patterns. When the American government was founded, despite the manors in Maryland, the estates of the patroons in New York, and the plantations in the South, the basic unit of American agriculture was the small freehold farm, and America was more than nine-tenths agricultural. At the end of the eighteenth century, the lives of the owner-operators of such farms were the typical American lives. The farmer was entrepreneur and laborer combined, and to a considerable extent self-sufficient, trading in surpluses only. By consequence, the values and forms of life were locally conceived, and discipline in respect to those values and forms was locally imposed. The wholeness of local life and its agricultural basis made the terms "farmer" and "citizen" seem synonymous. The farmer-citizen was in direct relationship with a government that was largely decentralized. Public policy was processed out of individual opinion at town meeting or county court; and the belief was generally held that government was democratized in proportion as it was localized.

The most characteristic of the institutions which America built for itself in the nineteenth

century, the democratic system of education, reflected this belief. The story is told of a writer
who visited the French Minister of Education
some thirty or forty years ago at eleven o'clock
in the morning. The Minister took out his watch
and said, "It is now eleven o'clock. Every boy
and girl of a certain grade in the public schools
of France is now studying this lesson," and
showed his visitor the lesson that they were studying. Such a story could not be told of American
education. American schools were started mainly
by the localities, townships, school districts, cities,
nor have they since been centralized in Washington.

Free education, freely accessible, is one of the
outstanding characteristics of the American style
of civilization, and one which, through its en-
couragement of study and debate and mutual
counsel, offers most promise toward the solution
of the difficulties ahead. For the problems that
Jefferson, Webster and Madison foresaw, in respect to property and in respect to democracy, are
now at hand. In the economic structure of today's
America, the life of the freehold farmer whom
those three men, in common with their generations, believed to be the main support of the
Constitution, is typical of only about half of the
agricultural population, and the agricultural

population is less than half of the nation as a whole.

The diffusion of economic decisions, characteristic of freehold farming, and the concentration of social values characteristic of compact community life are now minor features of the American tradition. The dominant patterns are reversals of the old designs for living: the concentration of economic decisions characteristic of industrial hierarchy and the diffusion of social values characteristic of nation-wide standardization.

The Jeffersonian ideal of an agrarian America definitely belongs to the past. That being so, the question then arises: Can democracy operate in a country whose manner of life and whose manner of making a living differ with all the difference between industry and agriculture? The farm affords the independent farmer opportunity for daily experience in policy-making; what has the factory to offer? Specialization, division of labor, has precluded the possibility of any one kind of life being typical of the America of today; what does that mean for the concept of the general welfare?

How serviceable in the present are the mainstays of the democracy of the American past? Freedom of speech, freedom of the press, freedom of assembly, freedom of teaching: How can

they be maintained in a world of teletype and
radio? Then there is that elusive concept which
nevertheless is perhaps the central concept of
American democracy, the concept of fair play.
American history, like American contemporary
life, does not lack for examples of the violation
of the fundamental civil liberties which were proclaimed in the early constitutional documents;
yet there has always been a general consensus that
it is the people's business to see that there is
fair play, and there have always been people who
were willing to fight for the right of all sides to
be heard and for the underdog to have his day.
The sense of fair play is probably America's best
guarantee that contemporary problems can be
solved within the limits of the law. But the sense
of fair play was developed in a society throughout which conditions were similar enough for
fair play to mean fair play between the various
members of one general group. How much harder
will its maintenance be in a society which specialization has divided into groups with different back-
grounds, different objectives, and insufficient in-
terchange of members for first-hand experience
of different types of group life to be very wide-
spread?

The importance of finding answers to these
questions is recognizable in proportion as it is
recognized that the position of early agriculture

and the circumstances of early democracy in the United States now belong to American history. For people primarily interested in agriculture, the ensuing problem is primarily a problem of finding the new role which the farm community has to play as a part along with other parts in the whole of the national life. For people primarily interested in democracy, the ensuing problem is a problem of discovering what conventions and institutions in the social structure of the past are inappropriate to present conditions, and what new conventions and institutions are necessary to the continuance of democracy in the contemporary world. But the two problems are closely interrelated, and answers to the questions put by those who concern themselves with the one are in considerable measure answers for those who concern themselves with the other. A search for such answers is the subject of the pages which follow.

CHAPTER II

APPLIED SCIENCE AND APPLIED FOLKWAYS

JEFFERSON, Webster and Madison foresaw the changes that came at the end of the era of free land. They could not foresee the changes that came at the beginning of the era of applied science. Yet at the very time when the closing of the frontier was confining American life within definite limits, new techniques were transforming the nature of American living.

Even on farms, the rhythm of daily experience, the routine of occupation, has altered at a revolutionary rate during the past two generations. Tractors, gang plows and combines, hard roads, trucks and autos, radio, electricity, have changed what the farm family does, the area over which it does it, and the radius of its communication with the world beyond the farm. The parallel changes in the city worker's life have been even greater, from the craftsman's shop to the endless belt, from the house to the flat, from distribution as a side-line of production to distribution as the sole occupation of six million people.

From the first rough-and-ready Yankee notion to today's hypersensitive photoelectric cell, no

American activity has received more consistent
social approval than the application of science to
practical ends. American society has generated to
an unusual degree the kind of pressure to which
throughout the ages the scientist has responded.
It was not by accident that the need for annual
resurveys of lands flooded by the Nile coexisted
with the rise of geometry in Egypt, nor that the
need for a calendar to warn of flood seasons in
Asia Minor coexisted with the rise of astrology
among the Chaldeans. The period of the great
voyages of discovery and the development of
astronomy, chronometers and clocks went together, and with the construction of these deli-
cate mechanisms came an understanding of some
of the fundamental principles of physical science.
As new continents were opened up and wealth
accumulated and labor grew scarce, the demand
for more goods than could be produced by hand
manufacture gave rise to machinery, and a rapid
advance in all branches of science accompanied
the filling of this need. The industrial revolution
created problems of ventilating mines, breweries
and the like and out of the resulting discoveries
concerning gases came the science of chemistry
and the key to the nature of matter.

Step by step, down the centuries, science and
society have moved along together. But they have
not always been in step at any particular time.

The research problem with which the scientist goes into his laboratory is more often than not related to a socially felt need. But the scientist gives no guarantee that he will come out of his laboratory with an answer to the need, or that if he does the answer will be what society wants. In fact, more often than not, the answer has disturbed or even shocked society—witness the treatment visited on such men as Galileo, Roger Bacon, Pasteur. The cultural effect of what the scientist turns out is unpredictable; the effect of scientific discovery on existing patterns of culture, both on customary ways of doing things and on customary ways of evaluating what is done, may be thoroughly disruptive.

The present time exhibits to an unusual degree the lack of balance between man and his physical environment and man and his society that may be occasioned by application of discoveries which were not predictable in terms of culture. One after another, the particular products forthcoming from the laboratories of applied science have received enthusiastic acclaim. As individuals, the American people have welcomed their cars, their radios, their labor-saving gadgetry of office, shop and kitchen; they have even exalted their bathtubs into symbols of the American standard of living. Collectively, the American people has joined in awed appreciation of its skyscrapers, its transcontinentals—streamlined, now, by rail and by air—its superhighways, as substantiation of the American dream that life should be bigger and better—and also more furious and fast. The conquest of space in the nineteenth century and the conquest of time in the twentieth have supplied the chief episodes of the American saga.

But in general, each new application of science has been considered as a separate episode. Each practical development has been regarded in terms of the immediate use for which it was intended. What of the sum total? What of the effect of these myriad new individual acts on society as a whole? From one point of view, the result of the application of science to make the automobile is the immediate convenience of the family that owns the car or the truck. But when looked at in terms of social effect, the result is expansion of the factory system, reorganization of the marketing of many products, increased construction of hard roads and decreased construction of railroads; enlargement of areas of government administration, including consolidation of the school system, loosening of family ties, and more besides.

The general effects of applied science have so far hardly been examined. Individual innovations go on, and in going on change the structure of society. At the same time the institutions built upon the previous social structure, the folkways that developed over long periods in the agricultural society preceding the industrial era, likewise continue to operate, in spite of the possibility that their original foundation in fact may have slipped out from under them and been replaced by something else.

A survey of recent developments related to scientific progress yields a formidable list of such changes, each affecting major institutions of American life.

Topping the list is the recent sudden increase in the capacity to produce, the result of a hundred years' pressure for usable, salable, city-made goods. Wanted: machinery to do the work. Invented: the technological basis for the modern factory system. Wanted: money to set up the machinery. Invented: the joint-stock company as a means of amassing the capital necessary for large-scale application of existing technology. Given: the profit motive as a basis of selection among available scientific data, a means of choice as to which of the new techniques should be translated from paper into concrete and steel and human energy, and eventual goods.

The management of the wealth, actual and potential, afforded by the new techniques presents the greatest of current problems to the United States and the rest of the industrialized world.

Throughout history, any sudden change in the quantity of wealth available for distribution, whether it be the diminishing supplies of the late Roman Empire or the glittering cargoes which the discoverers brought back from the new Indies and the old, has caused a crisis; and the transition from an economy where things are relatively few to an economy where things are potentially many is no exception. In America, moreover, where tradition has emphasized the economic structure to the near exclusion of other structural forms, social assumptions regarding the production and distribution of goods are peculiarly central.

To the founding fathers, property was an institution antecedent to government. The natural rights of man upon entering into the society, rights which government was set up to insure rather than to grant, were specified in the Declaration of Rights, as "life, liberty and the means of acquiring and possessing property and pursuing and obtaining happiness and safety." This announcement of the primacy of personal private property, legally guaranteed, was a matter of common accord among the men of the eastern seaboard who drafted the great constitutional documents. Among the men of the frontier, scattered like individual atoms over great distances, any institutional sense, whether of society, of property or of government, was necessarily vague, but the primary purpose of their westward passage was to obtain personal private property, through individual effort, by pre-emption. These parallel concepts of property were not the same; they were not, however, incompatible; and they became conjoint parts of the American tradition. But by the late nineteenth century two changes had rendered them insufficient: the passing of the frontier and the coming of the corporation.

Once the boundaries of the country were fixed, the pre-empted acres that had been treated like income became capital. Little by little the assumptions basic to their previous use began to be recognized as faulty assumptions in the new circumstances. As the natural resources of the country took on the appearance of a patrimony, whose present use was qualified by an obligation to hand it on unimpaired, a collective interest in management and maintenance began to emerge. A relationship between personal private property and the general welfare began to be perceived and to supplant the assumptions of the frontier tradition.

At about the same time, property-holding by corporations appeared alongside personal private property as a social fact of important dimensions for which a corresponding social concept was lacking. The corporation was the chartered creature of the government. To what extent was it a person? To what extent should it share the rights guaranteed to persons by the Constitution? Again old categories did not precisely fit; slowly old assumptions began to grow more inappropriate to new conditions.

And now, while the new social concepts of the relation of the general interest to the private use of national resources and the relation of government to industrial property right are still in the class of unfinished business, yet further alterations in the American concept of property, based on the increasing availability of goods, are clearly foreshadowed.

Contingent on the new ways of producing goods is mass insecurity. No earlier set of economic institutions, no earlier system of getting done the work of the world, has produced group insecurity on a comparable scale. Slaves were fed and housed. Feudal serfs might be equated with their lords' horses and cattle, but like the animals they were worth their stabling. Freehold farmers, in the era preceding commercial agriculture and one-crop farming, were to a large extent self-sufficient.

But the era of invention separated the process of manufacture and the process of distribution from the other activities of life. The industrial worker spends a certain number of hours a day in a factory. The white-collar worker spends a certain number of hours a day in an office. The operation of the factory and the office includes payment of wages when, as and if workers are needed. It includes no responsibility for their maintenance when not needed for the immediate execution of their work.

The position of commercial farmers has not been unlike that of factory and office workers. While the process of producing their crops has not been removed from the scene of the rest of their living, the marketing of agricultural products has become impersonal and remote, and fluctuations in demand have approximately the same effect on farm income as fluctuations in employment on the income of city workers.

Under such altered circumstances, rebuilding of traditional institutions for the provision of security by individuals, by private organizations, by government is clearly required. Rough and temporary scaffolding for such rebuilding has been run up by the commercial and industrial nations of the world in the form of emergency relief operations. More permanent structures have been begun under various laws for insurance, compensation and assistance. But full recognition of the strain on society which modern insecurity occasions has yet to be made.

In no aspect of social life has applied science wrought a greater revolution than in armaments. With munitions as they are currently manufactured, mass violence can be executed and mass intimidation produced by a fairly restricted number of people. No part of Jefferson's picture of America is more of an anachronism than his farmer with a flintlock as a symbol of national protection and self-defense. The old assumption that the security of a free state can be found in "a well-regulated militia" requires re-examination; applied science, through the armaments industry, has created a set of circumstances in which the second amendment to the Constitution is no longer a fully adequate statement. A new definition, expressing newly discovered social techniques, is requisite. If a few mechanized units can rout the spontaneous armies of the people, how shall policies regarding the use of the armed forces of the nation be made; how can protection against coercion—coercion at home or coercion from abroad—be best assured?

A further major change through which science is affecting society concerns the rapid alteration, since 1880, of the body of human knowledge. Two major forces in American society here combined. The wide diffusion of literate learning which followed the nineteenth-century inauguration of free education under public auspices was a revolutionary force; whenever in history there has been a sudden increase in the size of the group

possessed of such learning, alterations in the body
of knowledge itself have been a consequence. But
in this instance alteration of the body of knowledge because of the increased numbers among
whom it is shared has been paralleled by expansion of the body of knowledge through the sudden availability of scientific findings. Permeation
of these findings among the population has been
quickened by the extension of learning, and the
resulting social changes enormously enhanced.
Examples of such permeation are everywhere. In
the world of medical techniques, contraceptives
cut birth rates at the same time that death rates
are cut through combinations of sanitation, pre-
vention and cure. In the world of advertising,
mass appeals transmit news of inventions to the
four corners of the country. New customs and
new social strains are the result.

Parallel to such a list of innovations could be
put a list of traditional institutions which the innovations either have rendered, or are rendering,
obsolete. What about the institution of democracy? How compatible is democracy with the
other activities of modern society?

It is true that in the course of the history of
the Western world, from the Greek City states
down to the present, democracy has proved compatible with a wide variety of social and economic
arrangements, including the permutations of

three centuries of capitalism. But it is equally true that the division of labor has brought with it a separateness of experience whose implications for democracy are very grave indeed. At the manual level, the division of labor has gone on to such an extent that the majority of manual workers— except farmers—do not have the priceless privilege of making, at the same job, both a living and a life. At the intellectual level, the professionalization of skill has proceeded to the point of almost destroying a common language of communication between the several segments of mental work. Even among colleagues in a single profession, specialization is likely to go so far that no basis of sympathetic understanding exists within the group; the fissures between different professions, doctors and lawyers, teachers and engineers, are correspondingly broader.

But for those who have been able to exercise choice in selecting a profession, and have chosen well in terms of qualifications and temperamental bias, division of labor has made it possible for the individual man to become master of an order of happiness wherein mind and muscle are wedded in some type of extraordinarily skilled functioning. Such functioning is impossible except on the basis of a sufficiently minute division of labor to permit real mastery of the job with knowledge of its history and understanding of its ramifications,

so that the man commands the skill instead of
semi-skills commanding the man. Such a division
of labor gives that psychological unearned incre-
ment found in men who are happy at their work
and masters of the world over which they preside.
But it also carries the penalty that each of them
presides over so little, and is so desensitized to the
whole of life, that even two adjacent specialists
can hardly do more than speak to each other—and
often the less said the more understanding en-
gendered!

The fissures in the social fabric widen as larger
groups are considered. When all of the mental
workers are lumped together and called white-
collar people; when all of the manual workers
are lumped together in a conscious group; when
color, religion and other divisive categories are
recognized, the fissures widen into gullies and
chasms, and erosion of the soil in which democracy can grow takes place at a rapid rate.

In a society where the citizens are insensible to
one another's feelings and problems, democracy
becomes impossible: comradeship, fellowship,
friendship, even citizenship cease to be realities.
And most people, once they come to believe that
they are living in a culture from which unity has
departed, will desert that situation for any other
which convincingly claims to restore the tribal
sense of friendliness and comradeship in the

world. That primeval sense of human together-
ness has been so damaged by modern civilization
as to cause constant danger lest in mastering specialized work, citizens may achieve the good individual life to the death of the good society, may
be left with no social bond, no medium of communication, and no common kinesthesia to com-
municate to each other. Yet a continued capacity
to grasp the concept of the general welfare is essential to the maintenance of democracy in the
United States. The general welfare cannot have
meaning unless bridges are in operation across the
fissures and chasms of over-specialized living,
bearing constant traffic in exchange of the goods
which the various specialties have to offer. These
unearned increments of intensive living are the
objects of spiritual statesmanship.

The real problem of this age is the problem
of integrating the new forms of behavior which
have followed science into society. How can these
new forms of behavior be organized? Is it to be
done by individuals who arise and take on the
stature of heroes? What happens if institutions
existing from the previous period attempt to put
new behavior into a Procrustean bed of custom?
Can the conflict of interests be relied on to end
in a compromise which then becomes the social
norm? Is there a democratic process of organiz-

ing the new cultures of tomorrow? What are its principles and what its price?

The practice of democracy assumes the exercise of a certain amount of reason in the conduct of public affairs. What is the relation of reason to the new forms of social behavior which occur as new inventions start people doing things in ways other than the ways of the past? What is the relation of reason to the customs left over from old procedures? Is reason the systematizing of presumptions which arise irrationally out of movements in the social process, the canalizing of existing social forces?

The anthropologist believes that some of the questions about our own society can be answered by turning for a moment away from our own civilization and studying many independent and different societies. It is always possible that a society may be a special case, an exception that has never before occurred in the world, but it is far more likely that the mechanisms by which its members think and live are comparable with the mechanisms of other societies.

When Darwin studied the structure of beetles, he turned away from study of the skeleton of man and challenged the belief of his day that man was a special creation having nothing in common with the lower creations of the world. But in doing this, Darwin put human biology on a scientific

basis, gave it a new perspective, and laid the foundation for present-day knowledge of human or-
igin. Similarly, the anthropologist who studies
the Bella-Bella tribe or the Solomon Islanders
does not for a moment think that he is turning
away completely from his own society. He is
merely trying to get a scientific perspective on
the habits of people who live in groups. He goes
into their tribe and learns their language, lives
with them month after month, and records and
analyzes their life in the home, in the garden, on
the hunt, in the temple, at court. He is still primarily interested in his own civilization, but he
learns something about it by consulting a great
variety of specimens. He does not treat his own
society as a special case or as a final flowering. For
his purpose, the United States in 1939 is one
specimen, the Solomon Islanders another, the
Bella-Bella tribe another. All of these tribes, his-
torically unconnected with each other, are his
laboratory, in which he can get answers to questions as to what makes societies different, and
what institutions produce what results.

In the course of his investigations the anthropologist becomes highly skeptical of assertions
such as the one that "human nature" is unalter-
able. He observes that a comparison of various
cultures shows that certain kinds of "human
nature" develop under certain institutions; to

him, therefore, human nature is just a special set
of habits that have grown up in a special society
with special institutions.

He remarks that generation after generation
each society works for goals that are close to its
heart. Over larger and larger areas of life the tribe
keeps on co-ordinating its behavior in terms of
its major interests. Those interests may be war-
like and imperialistic, they may be peaceful and
domestic. They grow out of a long historic background, out of habits shaped partly by the mode
of production, partly by outside contacts with
other tribes, partly by the accident of the kind of
persons who achieve prestige in the tribe, whether
they are priests or men of property, warriors or
gamblers.

The habits of the tribe become a mold which
shapes each oncoming generation of children; if,
by chance, individual members of the tribe pursue eccentric goals or develop extreme habits of
behavior they are, after all, cut short at the end
of their threescore years and ten. No such finis,
however, is written to the behavior of the tribe
as a whole. Generation after generation it can
pursue curious goals and develop bizarre habits
of behavior. Indeed the customs which societies
defend most passionately as natural and socially
desirable are usually those which in the eyes of
an outside observer seem least suited to the con-

ditions to which they are applied. They are the
last things which societies will submit to critical
analysis; even though the dominant assumptions
of a given society are wholly unsuited to the circumstances of some or all of its members, they
are characteristically accepted without examination and defended with warmth.

Examples of such acceptance and defense may
be cited from widely varying incidents of social
organization, from procedures concerning sex,
concerning the training of children, concerning
property. Some tribes regard nothing as important except their collective activities: their corporate existence as a tribe, their cult societies,
their rain magic, their calendric ritual. Nothing
that concerns the individual is of much interest
to them. Marriage may be relatively permanent
even in such tribes, but it is a private matter. It is
not something with which the tribe as a whole is
concerned. The fact that the tribe is preoccupied
with corporate affairs rather than the lives of individuals likewise affects behavior at death: fu-
nerals are simple affairs to put grief out of the
way, as they say, in one day. The centering of life
around major interests is equally characteristic of
many tribes which value property above everything else. Such tribes marry property, they
mourn property, they estimate insults in terms of
property. Property dominates their religion and

their art. As one of these tribes says, "Never harbor kindly feelings; it costs too much."

The extent to which anti-social behavior dictated by tribal customs may nonetheless receive vigorous approval from all members can be illustrated by the marriage customs of certain Australian tribes. In those tribes it is forbidden for a man to marry anyone who is related to him through his father, or anyone remotely related to his father, or through his mother, or anyone remotely related to his mother, or anyone in his locality. Since the tribes are small groups of some two hundred people, the point is soon reached where no man may marry. Nevertheless a man runs off with a girl. Then all his family and hers follow them with clubs and spears. They track them down if possible, and if they catch them they kill them. If the young couple escape, they take refuge on an island which is a kind of sanctuary. There they must stay until they have a child. After their baby is born, they can return to the tribe, but in returning they are met by all their relatives fully armed. The tribe sets upon them with spears and clubs, spearing them and beating them until they are well bloodied and black and blue. Then the young couple may settle down as a married pair. Yet every man and woman in the tribe who has thrown a spear, every man and woman in the tribe who has wielded a club on this couple has himself and herself been married in exactly the same way. But the tribe does not relax its rules; its definition of incest remains the same. Its members do not see that such behavior is anti-social; it is the way of life to which they are accustomed and they defend it passionately. Instances of this sort are by no means unusual.

Customary procedure that bears no necessary relation to the facts to which it is applied is equally plentiful in the realm of economic shibboleths. The effect of man-made institutions on economic welfare is particularly striking in cases where neighboring tribes use diametrically opposite economic patterns in dealing with the same natural resources. In one tribe the mechanism of distribution may be such as to funnel all the goods of life to the rich, so that wealth has only one prime destination—the person already endowed with valuable possessions. In another tribe, economic organization may be so arranged as constantly to siphon wealth away from points of concentration.

Funnel societies depend upon ownership of means of production and the right of favored persons to corner certain articles of wealth. They reach their highest development where interest is an institution and where wealth can be used to obtain forced labor; but they are found among peoples of widely varied occupations, simple hoe

agriculturalists, reindeerherders, modern industrialists, and even poverty-stricken food gatherers
in the South Seas, whose economic rivalry takes
the form of heaping up food and ostentatiously
letting it rot, the proportions of the stench hang-
ing heavy over the village symbolizing the magni-
tude of the victory over the neighbors.

The mechanism of siphon societies takes the
form of work bees or of great giveaways which
bring honor and poverty to the owner. The work
of the tribe is done in a manner comparable to
the cornhusking parties of older America; all
comers are fed and go home carrying food, and
everyone reciprocates with help in another's
fields. The older generation also sets up the boys
and girls with the goods they need; the young do
not wait for the death of their elders. The fact
that the young man and the young woman are
now able to work is reason enough, in the eyes of
the tribesmen, for them to have tools and capital
to work with, since everything they produce en-
hances the wealth of the tribe. At the giveaways
a man's prestige is established not by what he has
left but by what he has parted with. In such societies a father teaches his son, "You see me here.
I am renowned above all men. I have nothing.
Go also and become poor and you too will be a
great man among our people." Like funnel so-

cieties, siphon societies are found at opposite ends of the earth, from Africa to the Siberian plains.

Study of the folkways of many tribes serves to open the eyes of the anthropologist to the folklore of capitalism as currently practiced in the United States. Trained through comparative observation, he considers with interest the symbolic ritual through which the governing concepts of the economic system are expressed. He remembers that in other communities, the most passionate defense was usually reserved for the most bizarre institutions, for the habits and customs which rational consideration found most inappropriate to the purpose which they were alleged to perform. The more a given way of doing things is proclaimed as a sacred universal human right, the more the anthropologist will suspect that critical examination is needed. When he hears, in the America of 1939, that human nature demands a free field for competition, that human nature demands that the individual be free to regulate all his affairs without interference, he will remember that human nature in many societies has been almost spectacularly co-operative and that the societies have been highly stable and satisfactory. He will likewise have learned to discriminate between inspirational statements of tribal objectives and the performance which they symbolize—he will read the block-long motto carved above the

New York Post Office, "Neither Storm, nor Rain, nor Snow, nor Gloom of Night, Stays These Couriers in the Swift Completion of Their Appointed Rounds," and realize that this means that mail will be delivered even in bad weather.

Institution by institution he will turn from the official portrait, taken with the subject in full regalia, and look at—or if none is available, make— an anatomical chart. From the official portraits he will learn what features have the collective approval of the American people and what trappings fulfill the traditional ceremonial expectations of this particular society. And then from the anatomical charts he will estimate the appropriateness of existing social regalia to the functions which the charts indicate the living organisms beneath are fitted to perform.

Studies of a wide variety of organized societies supply material which contemporary movements may use as resources of the first order. Just as Darwin's findings on the skeletal structure of beetles had much to contribute to the understanding of human anatomy, and thus to medical art, the findings of the cultural anthropologist have much to contribute to the understanding of modern society and thus to the strategy of those interested in current adaptations of the democratic technique.

The science of man provides a basis for a sense

of continuity of human experience in a world where discontinuity and contemporaneity have been receiving a disproportionate share of attention. From instant to instant, other sciences are causing changes which lead modern Americans to say, "In the old days," "In the horse and buggy era," "Before the War," or "Way back a hundred years ago," and mean a time when habits and customs were so different from the habits and customs of today as to make the men and women of that time seem like strangers to, rather than immediate ancestors of, the Americans of the present. The science of man is a force in the opposite direction. Its findings are in terms not of moments but of millenia; they show the relatedness of men living over thousands of years under myriad different conditions, on all of the continents of the globe. The sense of man's adaptability, the reassurance of a long line of succession, with the hand of one generation on the shoulder of the next, is important to an age whose feeling of isolation is one factor in its sense of bewilderment.

Anthropology is thus capable of fulfilling somewhat the same function in respect to human society that Darwin's studies fulfilled in demonstrating a structural continuity from species to species. Appreciation of the fact that certain common characteristics are shared by all sorts of societies in turn provides the basis for comparisons be-

tween social structures, and these comparisons
supply contemporary movements with certain important premises.

One major premise is that the dynamics of men
acting together in groups is the source of most of
the momentum through which traditional modes
of behavior are perpetuated or innovations introduced. Appreciation of the central importance of
group life serves to correct the individualistic assumptions which political democracy has tended
to bring with it down the years from the time of
laissez-faire.

The growing importance of group life is a matter of particular importance to farmers, whose
occupation has tended to keep them separate from
other members of their group more than most
other major occupations in the nation. Around
what different activities should the group life of
the farm community be organized for the expression of farm interests—by communities, by regions, nationally? What types of organization,
public and private, are required? How can the
groups organized around farm interests become
aware of the interests of other groups, and convey
their own interests to them, and to the nation at
large? How can democracy best be practiced in
and among these groups?

A second major premise which contemporary
movements may derive from the findings of cul-

tural anthropology concerns the importance of dramatic mythology in giving unity and a sense of direction to the members of a social group. This premise has certain very definite corollaries for those who are attempting to co-ordinate established folkways and new behavior: since in all tribes even a slight change in customary procedure is apt to be looked upon as a veritable revolution, new proposals must find their acceptability through being related to existing formulae for doing things.

A current example of such a process is to be found in the operation of the recent soil erosion programs in the American Southwest. The culture of the Navajo Indians includes economic patterns developed out of their own tradition. Property is passed on in matrilineal descent. Families hold their property on the basis of combined ownership and use—if a family lets a piece of land lie idle, another family that is prepared to render it productive can occupy it without protest. In the sheepherding operations which form a major economic activity, groups of families make various contributions to the operations of herding, shearing and butchering, and share in the total result by a complicated system of customary arrangements.

The economic pattern of the white man's society has conflicted with the traditional Navajo culture at all of these points, and the disruption of custom which has followed contact with white men has caused characteristic social strains. Increase of the herds and disappearance of their range through overgrazing and drought has produced parallel economic strains. In these circumstances the inauguration of a soil conservation program presents exceptional difficulties, and difficulties whose solution can be considerably aided through an anthropological approach.

A first requirement of success in incorporating into Navajo activities the findings of scientific technicians is to find a proper Indian group with which to negotiate. The Navajos do not have a unified tribal structure with a hierarchy of chieftains—in previous negotiations the choice of leaders to act as representatives has been made by the white groups desiring to negotiate. Furthermore, while the tribal leadership has come from the men, the property concerning which they have made agreements belongs not to them but to the women of the tribe.

A second task is to find a common language of communication. Such phrases as "carrying capacity" or "overstocking" represent technical concepts which have no counterpart in Navajo thought. Literal translation therefore conveys only words; understanding requires transmission of ideas.

These conditions are conditions in which the way to success lies along the paths of the social sciences. The expert in soils and the expert in animal husbandry have a primary contribution to make toward an improved economic status for this group in American agriculture. But the social scientists must play a role of comparable importance if the program is to represent a process not of imposing an alien pattern on a people given no choice, but a process in which that people shares, a process in which proper consideration is given alike to applied science and to applied folkways.

Appreciation of the importance of integrating current economic programs with existing folkways in a culture which differs from the prevalent American culture as much as that of the Navajos has a transferable value in relation to the general agricultural activities of the American scene. Anthropological studies indicate the extent to which the folkways that attract group allegiance may be provincial, may even be so inappropriate to current circumstances as to defeat the purpose for which they exist. It therefore becomes pertinent to ask: To what extent is that true of what assumptions in contemporary American society? What are the ruling images of the good life in the United States? Are those images supplied by one group and acceded to by other groups to whose

circumstances they are less fitting—do farmers, for
instance, tend to accept and make their own certain designs for living manufactured in the cities
and little suited to rural culture? The image of
the good life as the life of the rich man character-
izes all societies whose economy is the funnel type
—what meaning does that have for the farmer in
a democracy? And to what extent do the group
antagonisms typical of funnel societies set American farmers against American factory workers to
the detriment of the welfare of both?

On the other hand, anthropological studies also
show how the power of societies to strive for and
successively attain their major objectives may be
enhanced by common devotion to a common belief as to nature of the general welfare. Against a
background of comparative studies, the search for
a democratic means of ordering and organizing
the new behavior which has followed science into
society is recognized as being in no small measure
a continuing search for a common belief, commonly understood, that the citizens of the United
States can live and die for. There are several parts
to the belief: one includes the civil liberties; one
includes a measure of economic security; one includes the sense of fair play that affirms the social
value of differences, that sees democratic history
as the progress of minorities which were heard,

and were persuasive enough to convert the majorities hearing them.

Each of these parts has continually to be newly defined in terms of new day-to-day activities, and newly related to the whole. The procedure of redefinition is the democratic process, and the living result is a society in which democratic aims have become the goals. The necessity of such a belief is apparent if the complex forces in American life are to be organized for democracy. And it is equally apparent that the absence of belief in democracy leaves the way open to competing ideologies for collective living.

CHAPTER III

THE WAY OF DICTATORSHIP

CLEARLY, the democratic technique is facing increasing competition. The type of political system which before 1914 seemed the norm toward which all countries were progressing is today confined to a diminishing number of governments, and the problems which democracies are struggling to solve, notably the relationships of farm and city and the relationships of capital and labor, are in other countries being attacked by other methods.

It is pertinent to look at the operation of these other systems for two reasons: because their problems are sufficiently like the major problems of the United States to admit of comparison, and because what they do nationally and internationally in turn affects what can be done by and in the United States.

From one point of view, it seems unjustified to consider the dictatorships of Russia, Germany and Italy together, so deep is the contrast between them. The conflict between the Soviet Union, with its communist ideology, and the Fascist powers, with their concepts of nation and race, is perhaps the gravest problem in Europe and in the world today. The Russian Revolution was a revolution led by the industrial classes of the cities and supported by the workers out in the country. Their slogan was, "World Revolution for the Workers," anti-capitalism in the strict Marxian sense, the idea of a classless society, equalitarian and world-wide. The German and the Italian movements, particularly in their beginnings, were mainly movements of the lower middle class, turning violently against the Marxian labor movement. Anti-Marxism was one of their main slogans. They aimed to awaken the nation against internationalism, particularly against communist world revolution; they differed profoundly from the Communists in their views on property and on practically everything else in their society.

But if these movements are regarded from the point of view of the democracies, they are found to share most of the governmental and economic characteristics in which they differ from democracy. Their techniques of government are all very similar. Each operates under a dictatorial system conducted by one party with no open opposition. In Russia and in Germany the technique of mass propaganda has been developed to great heights. The importance of the individual, the private citizen, is denied; citizens and individuals exist to serve the State. These assumptions negate most of the social ideals that have been regarded as the valuable achievements of Western civilization.

But why should these countries have turned with such violence against the ideals and institutions built up by the earlier organized countries of the Western world? Before discussing the answer, it might be mentioned that each of them claims in a way to be more closely akin to the Western world than the other. The Communists claim that they are willing to help the democracies save civilization from the Fascists, and that many of their ideals are more intimately related to those of the democracies than the Fascist ideals —they are pacifists and internationalists and universalists. The Fascists claim that they are calling the world to follow their leadership in fighting what they consider the archthreat to civilization, Bolshevism from the East. Thus in a way both are trying to gain the sympathies of the West and trying to form some kind of union across the gulf that they have created between their own governmental system and social philosophy and that of the democracies.

But why then should they differ so fundamentally from the democracies? They have a certain common background that explains some of the difference. The postwar revolutions occurred in countries that had never been countries of parliamentary democracy or Western individualism.

Russia and the rest of Central Europe and Germany were in their structure up to the end of the War what one might call pre-capitalist or feudal; particularly Russia, of course, but Germany also. Theirs was not a civilization built on the ideas that have come down from the French and American revolutions. It was a civilization in which no counterpart of Jeffersonian democracy had ever existed. The result can be seen in the reaction that occurred in those countries after the War.

The Russian Revolution called itself a Marxian labor revolution against capitalism, but in Russia there was little capitalism as the Western nations know it. Fundamentally it was an anti-feudal revolution against the big landowners, following which the industrial workers in the cities began to build up the industry which did not exist before. The industrial workers have always been a relatively small minority relying for support on the landless proletariat out in the open country on the feudal estates.

In Germany, too, the revolution which brought Hitler into power was not a counterrevolution of the big industrialists against labor, as Marxists have tried to make the world believe. Hitler had fourteen million adherents before he got into power, a number which could not be accounted for by any means at the disposal of the capitalists. While some industrialists certainly sympathized

with the Nazi party and gave it their backing, it
arose from a mass movement of the lower middle classes in Germany—the broad lower middle
classes that include the millions and millions of
farmers and retailers and small shopkeepers—and
the large bureaucracy, and the army, and the people who were still living from handicraft, and
much of the white-collar proletariat. These clung
to many of the ideals of the past, and to them the
Marxist labor movement was a symbol of the de-
cay of their old society. In many ways they re-
sented the development of modern capitalism as
much as the workers did; they were both anti-
capitalist and anti-Marxist. To them the Versailles
Treaty was the great symbol of disaster abroad;
the Weimar Republic which succeeded the im-
perial government in Germany seemed a domestic
indication of the destruction of what they had
clung to. And in addition to these political
changes, the War and the subsequent inflation
destroyed their economic security and their welfare. Out of that situation, out of a background
totally different from that of the democracies, and
out of emergency, defeat and revolution, grew
this tremendously powerful, violent and militant
mass movement, the anti-Communist mass movement of National Socialism. In Italy the situation
was very similar although the movement did not
muster quite the support that was available in

Germany from those who had suffered defeat and revolution and inflation.

Thus there is the world of the dictatorships and the world of the democracies, and the former split in two by a profound hostility; the world in which there is still the outlook of individualistic and democratic civilization and the world in which fighting organisms have taken hold of all economic and political life and incorporated the individual in a way which leaves him practically no sphere of his own.

With their completely different philosophy and outlook, how have these new organizations tried to grapple with the problems of the twentieth century? In a way they have not had to grapple with the same, but with other problems. Russia has not been dealing with a highly developed capitalistic society; rather she has been building one. Industrialization was a nineteenth-century problem in the democracies; to the extent that the Russians are building industries, they are only picking up and developing the two main problems with which the democracies have now to deal, the problems of urban society and the problems of the relationship of urban society to the farmers.

Though Germany is an industrial country, many of her problems are also in a class by themselves. She is facing the problems of an emergency that dates from the War and the postwar period, a situation in which she cannot get the foreign exchange needed to buy essential foodstuffs and raw materials. And secondly, she is facing the problems of a military economy. While not the central feature of the ideology of the National Socialist regime, this military economy is taking hold of Germany more and more, and is perhaps in practice the outstanding reality today in the life of the German people.

By military economy is meant an economy whose main purpose is to give the country enough self-sufficiency so as to not be starved in the next war. All countries are devoting enormous energy trying to win the last war or to keep out of the last war; that is to say, a war identical with the last war. The general staffs are trying to do the things which they should have done before 1914; the economic staffs are trying to do the things which, if they had been able to do them before 1914, would have made the situation better in the years that followed. In Germany the main problem is how to stand the pressure of a blockade like the one that brought on the defeat of the last war. That is the central theme of the four-year plan and of all German economic policy, industrial and agricultural; to build up a basis of food supplies sufficient to keep alive during a war. The plan accepts the sacrifice of a large part of German peacetime prosperity in order to have the minimum needed to keep going through a next war which is visualized as strategically like the last.

Over and above the problems of self-sufficiency and scarcity of foreign exchange, however, the Germans are also having to face the problems which every industrial country is facing; and it is pertinent to see what they have been doing in the realms in which democracies are finding their most important economic issues.

In the industrial field two issues stand out today over and above all others: one is the relationship between labor and capital; the other, the problem of unemployment. With regard to labor and capital, the solution proposed by the Russians is the most radical one—do away with the capitalists and there are no problems. That, however, remains to be proved. While some of the problems seem at least temporarily to have disappeared, the management of socialized capitalism in Russia may create problems which were believed to have been abolished with private ownership.

The German solution, or the Fascist solution in Italy, is not simply a reversal of the Russian, not simply a solution in favor of capital, in favor of the small minority that owns the means of production. Labor cannot be abolished; a large industrial force is indispensable. The theory of the

Fascist solution is this: get the two classes, the
property-owning class and labor, to forget their
differences, or at least to regard them as minor
issues, and find something in common which
seems so important that former differences become secondary; link them together in a common
nationalism, a feeling for the national community, an enthusiasm for the policy of the nation
as a whole, which will perhaps make the economic
problems into minor issues. In practice this solution also meant taking from the two groups the
power to fight for their particular interests. Since
that involved stabilizing wages and profits as they
were at the time, many people have said that the
bargain was utterly at the expense of labor. But
if it had been only at the expense of labor, it
could have done nothing toward solving the problem. The other part of the bargain was the establishment of a government machine over both
classes which gave some satisfaction to labor in
the knowledge that a limit was being put on capital's chances of profit. The Fascist and National
Socialist solution, however, is largely an ideological one. The difficulties attendant on profit economies make a more fundamental solution very
difficult, for the pressure on capitalists and en-
trepreneurs, while constant, is less severe than the
concomitant reductions in the income of the
masses.

As in the case of Russia, it is too soon to estimate the adequacy of the way in which the Fascist countries are seeking a solution of the problem of capital and labor. It is possible that the
feudal background which lay immediately behind
their industrialization emphasized their class consciousness and weakened the tendency for any
kind of co-operation to develop; that background
too may be the source of the desire to put above
these warring classes an instrument of power
strong enough to keep each in its place.

If the Communist and National Socialist solutions of the problem of capital and labor are still
in doubt, what of their respective attacks on the
problem of unemployment? Germany had six million unemployed at the depth of the depression,
but in the last few years both Germany and Russia have performed what appears like a miracle—
they have no unemployed to speak of. The solution in Russia has been found in the constant
boom of industrialization to the point where there
has even been a shortage of industrial labor. In
Germany, the solution that has been found is the
one which every other country has tried to a
greater or lesser extent, namely, public expenditure. Such use of public funds raises the double
question: How long can it be continued, and what
chance is there of it becoming unnecessary? By a
tragic paradox, rearmament has everywhere pro-

vided a way out of economic depression, and nowhere more so than in Germany. But since nations cannot forever continue to rearm or con-
struct roads or build pyramids, the point at which
their tremendous programs of public expenditure
will be replaced by private investment as a means
of absorbing the unemployed becomes important
to find. If private investment does not take place,
will governments have to shift their public works
programs more and more into the fields of normal productive enterprise? In Italy private capital seems to be disappearing from the field; if
accumulated it goes to the government for investment. The end of such a move would seem to be
national monopoly, whether desired or undesired.

The other major modern problem is the relationship between farm and city. Each country
with no exception is facing the problem of the
distribution of national income between the agricultural population and the producers in the city,
and this problem is no less fundamental and no
less difficult to grapple with than the problem of
the relation between capital and labor.

Marxian theory contains very little on the subject: the old Marxian conception assumed that
there was only one problem, labor and capital,
ignoring the large middle-class groups, particularly out in the country, that were neither capitalists nor proletarian industrial workers. Yet the

agrarian problem was among the first problems that the Russian Revolutionaries had to face.

There has never been a successful revolution backed only by people in the cities; neither revolution nor counterrevolution comes about unless backed by the producers in agriculture, by the farmers or the peasants. That is true for Germany and true for Russia; it was true for the French Revolution and the American. In the countries of the Western world, the farmers have been and are today the backbone of democracy. Those countries in Europe that are safely democratic are democratic because their farmers are democratic; countries like France or Switzerland, or Denmark or Sweden; countries that have farmers who cling to the ideals of individual property and individual freedom. In the countries which have given up democracy the rural population either had no tradition of democracy or turned against the democratic ideals it had held.

Some people believe that the Russian farmers one day will turn to farm democracy; their backing of the Communist Revolution was after all based on the hope of gaining individual property. But due to the subsequent dominance of industrial Marxist labor in the Russian state, the individual holdings which farmers obtained at the time of the Revolution were collectivized. After the campaign against the kulaks under Stalin some sixty percent of the farmers pooled their lands in collective farms.

In Germany, the farmers backed the National Socialist Revolution for many reasons. The German farmer was one of the most important elements in the social and political structure of the old regime in Germany. He was a traditionalist, a nationalist, strongly in favor of the kind of government that Germany had before the War. He thoroughly disliked the change that came about in 1918, not because it gave Germany democracy but because it brought the government into the hands of city groups which he could not understand and which had little understanding for his problems. Under the Weimar Republic the mood of the farmers deteriorated into a mood in which they were willing to back anything that would call itself anti-Marxist and promise to save Germany from humiliation and restore the lost power and glory of the country.

Unlike the Soviet, the National Socialist State has maintained and even stressed individual landholding, but the one phase of German economic life which can today be called socialist is the "nutritionist state," the agricultural life of the country. Farm income has been raised at the expense of the rest of the population; debts have been reduced; and a variety of other measures taken to aid the farmer. At the same time farm produc-

tion, prices and marketing have become the subject of thoroughgoing government control.

In both Italy and Germany, agricultural control is at the center of the program of self-sufficiency. Under government direction, certain specific objectives have been rapidly reached. In both
countries the "battle of wheat" has been a rapid
victory, quickly carried out. But the problem is
not only a matter of giving the Italians enough
wheat to produce their bread; it is a matter of
making them less dependent on foreign exchange
with which to buy foodstuffs, and where wheat
production has been substituted for eggs and
butter and even cattle, imports of these latter
goods have risen. In Germany, the wartime lack
of fats was at least as great as the lack of bread.
Yet increased wheat acreage has cut pasturage and
fodder production, and forced an increased dependence on foreign fats and feed. It therefore
appears that there is at least a tendency for particular successes in one sector to cause gaps in
others and lead to new efforts which again throw
the burden elsewhere.

The difference in prerevolutionary background
between the countries that have become totalitarian since the War and the democracies, and the
extent to which the dictatorship countries have
had their own peculiar emergencies and military
problems to face, limits the comparability of the

techniques they have used and the success they have obtained in dealing with the problems that they share alike with all industrialized countries. Yet there is a basis for some comparison: farm programs, public works as a stimulant to private enterprise, and general economic planning are common phenomena of major interest in democratic countries. Moreover, the experience of the totalitarian states has a further importance. The fact that these revolutions happened is a warning to the democracies.

In their efforts to avoid the distress and regimentation of dictatorships, the democracies may find protection in studying the forces that led to the creation of dictatorial systems in other countries. The totalitarian revolutions may possibly be looked upon as a forecast of what might happen if labor-capital relations in the cities should develop into class war, instead of co-operation, or if the city and rural populations could not come to terms and the farmers got the impression that the class war in the cities was being solved at their expense. Another conjecture is that if the farmers should get the impression that the government is not theirs, the unrest and revolt in rural districts might possibly be taken advantage of by one of the fighting parties in the industrial sphere. A further possibility might be that the techniques of the proletarian and middle-class uprising might be grasped by groups which do not have mass movements to back them. The experience of other nations indicates that the nature of modern armaments increases the capacity of military dictatorships to get into power and then obtain plebescitary approval from masses that find themselves without a choice.

The existence of the technique of dictatorship as a widely used alternative to the democratic process is in itself a challenge to the present American system of government. It is a challenge whose insistence is greatly increased by the fact that most of the dictatorships are on the march. What are the chances of American democracy surviving if the rest of the world becomes totalitarian or engages in a general war?

If the United States again goes to war, it might be necessary, as it seemed to be necessary in 1917, temporarily to replace some of the democratic institutions of the country with more dictatorial processes. National leaders have felt that only through these instruments of control can the national resources be adequately mobilized for war purposes. Recognition of the prospects of dictatorial methods may be a main factor in the isolationist sentiment of the country, and may account for much of the interest and support which various neutrality measures have received in the course of the past few years. But there is need for

examination of the other assumption on which
this interest and support is based, namely, that if
the United States remains out of a war raging in
the Orient and Europe and eventually Latin
America, civil liberties and democratic institutions can be maintained within her borders.

In case of war, a policy of genuine isolation
would require the cutting of economic ties with
the outside world and the rapid establishment of
a basis for economic self-containment. The loss of
foreign markets following the last war has imposed upon the government a gigantic task of intervention in the economic process, particularly
in agriculture; but present efforts in that direction would pale into insignificance if thoroughgoing economic self-containment became the objective of government effort. The countries which
have made the greatest effort toward self-sufficiency are the dictatorships of Italy and Germany.
The people of the United States are therefore
faced with the paradox that complete isolation
requires an economic system which in other countries has been established by authoritarian measures.

Furthermore, it is a question whether neutrality can be maintained without control of public
opinion. Tensions in the next war, as its prelim-
inary phases have made clear, are bound to be
more acute, more divisive, than in the last. Ameri-

cans are people of opinion and emotional reaction, and the need for a policy of censorship which might be felt by a government bent on maintaining neutrality has even now been indicated.

Censorship of movies relating to war issues has already been exercised; the Neutrality Act prohibits Americans from making contributions to belligerent governments; in 1938, Congress passed legislation prohibiting the picketing of Washington embassies which was attacked by conservative newspapers as violation of freedom of speech.

Grave difficulties would therefore appear to attend an effort to build an isolated island of democratic sentiment in a world at war. And if American democracy cannot maintain itself by turning its back on the international scene, it becomes vitally important to estimate the strengths and weaknesses of the way of democracy in a world situation where the way of dictatorship is increasingly setting the pace. Is democracy capable of adopting and following a foreign policy that will avert war?

The difficulty of the American people as a whole developing, in any organized sense, concepts of policy based on enlightened self-interest and intelligence is probably greater in the field of foreign than in that of domestic policy for two reasons: both the technique by means of which

foreign policy is made, and the questions to which
the technique is applied present problems in democratic control.

When it comes to agriculture, Congress defines
a general mandate and it is the function of the
Department of Agriculture to carry it out. The
situation in regard to foreign policy is entirely
different. Ever since the debate between Hamilton and Madison over the first Neutrality Proc-
lamation of 1800, it has been legally established
that in all matters of foreign policy not expressly
reserved to Congress the President, as part of his
prerogative, has control.

Executive determination of foreign policy was
taken over from British constitutional law under
which matters of foreign policy are part of the prerogative of the Crown. But the difference between
the remaining features of the constitutions of the
two countries has served greatly to enhance the
relative power of the American President. The
British Prime Minister, the French Premier, are
subject to question and debate on the floor of the
House of Commons and the Chamber of Deputies,
and an adverse vote of those representative bodies
overthrows them. The principle of the separation
of powers prevents similar democratic control in
the United States. The question of whether the
American Navy shall be sent for service in the
Atlantic or the Pacific is a matter for the President

alone to decide. The question of whether a protest should be lodged because of the sinking of an American ship or the death of an American national or because of an alleged violation of international law is a matter of presidential discretion.

The provision that the President shall make treaties with the advice and consent of two-thirds of the members present in the Senate originated as a necessity of the domestic politics of the Constitution-making period rather than as a means of giving power to the legislative arm in the conduct of foreign relations. Fear that treaties, as part of the supreme law of the land, would be used to break down States' rights, particularly fear of the power of the large states on the part of the small states, and fear on the part of the states of the Mississippi and Ohio valleys as to the effect of territorial agreements made without their consent, was sufficient to account for the original provision. The development of the party system further obscured the operation of this provision. Although the Senate was intended originally to be a non-partisan advisory body, votes giving or withholding consent to presidential foreign policy usually reflect partisan considerations. Thus the President has been given the widest discretion in every matter of foreign policy except the actual consummation of treaties, while the Senate has been given veto power over treaty arrangements.

In recent years, various efforts have been made to reduce the frequency of partisan deadlock between the executive and the Senate, and at the same time to provide a larger voice in foreign policy for the legislative branch of the government.

One of these has been appointment of Senators as members of delegations attending conferences and negotiating treaties, on the assumption that they would not allow provisions to be inserted which, in their opinion, the Senate will subsequently reject. On the whole, however, this measure has had only qualified success, since the senatorial delegates have frequently found themselves regarded on their return as spokesmen of the Administration, and therefore without the independent influence they would otherwise enjoy.

A device which has been increasingly used, and which eliminates senatorial concurrence entirely, is that of the Executive Agreement, whereby an exchange of notes covering an agreed course of action takes place between the head of the American government and that of another power. Probably the most famous early example of this technique was the gentlemen's agreement made during the presidency of Theodore Roosevelt under which Japan agreed not to issue passports to immigrants to the United States, an agreement terminated rather abruptly by Congress in 1924. More recently, as a form of executive discretion under general legislation originating with Congress, agreements have been substituted for treaties under the reciprocal trade program of Secretary Hull.

A second substitute for the two-thirds vote required for senatorial ratification of treaties, and one which will probably be used more in the future, is the Joint Resolution of both Houses of Congress. This was the method used when the United States joined the International Labour Organization; had it been employed earlier, the United States would have been a member of the World Court and might conceivably have had a more responsible relationship to other international organizations.

Against the background just outlined, various proposals have been advanced in the last few years with the object of democratizing the conduct of America's foreign policy.

Most drastic is the proposed Ludlow amendment under which, unless the United States were being actually invaded, Congress would be prohibited from declaring war until it had taken a plebiscite. The recent history of plebiscites, however, has caused many people to question their usefulness.

An alternative proposal is amendment of the Constitution to substitute a majority of both

Houses of Congress for the present Senate requirement on treaties. While theoretically there is
everything to be said for this technique, the practical difficulties of securing the passage of an
amendment are formidable.

Among less formal arrangements, two proposals
recommend themselves. One is for the appointment by the President of an Advisory Committee
on Foreign Affairs, containing representatives of
the committees of the House and the Senate, for
the constant consideration of foreign policy both
during and between sessions of Congress. The
other provides that the Secretary of State and
other Cabinet officers, whose respective fields are
involved, shall appear at stated times on the floor
of Congress to answer questions and defend their
foreign policies in regular debate. The former
suggestion would provide for regular participation
by the legislative branch of the government during the formative period of policy-making. The
latter would provide the check on executive discretion by popular representatives which exists in
the other democratically organized states.

Aside from the technical obstacles to democratic participation in the making of foreign policy offered by the peculiarities of the American
Constitution, however, there are other difficulties
due to the very nature of the subjects with which
foreign policy has to deal. In the first place, the in-

ternational questions of this complicated age are
even more complicated than the domestic questions. In addition, international questions lack
even as much of the atmosphere of rationality as
is available for domestic questions. Foreign affairs is a field in which slogans and symbols are
perhaps less analyzed than any other. Attack on
the foreigner is a stock in trade which has brought
applause to many a politician, for people are apt
to distrust what they do not understand, and it is
difficult for any large number of citizens to get
to know the traditions, the differences, the idiosyn-
crasies of the countries which American foreign
policy must take into account.

In all of the democracies, general moral convictions with regard to international conduct, convictions concerning the necessity for justice, the im-
morality of war, the desirability of peace, are fer-
vently held. These general convictions are, however, unrelated to specific policies and specific actions. Governments of the countries where they
are held are consequently under two types of pressure. They have continually to take specific action
in furtherance of specific policies and yet they are
the prisoners of this general public opinion.

It is difficult for the mass opinion of a democracy to perceive, and then follow out, the necessary steps to give concrete recognition to its general ideas. When public opinion says of a con-

quest: "This conquest flouts every principle of international behavior. We will never recognize it, and we will castigate the dictator who did it," the government guided by that opinion can do nothing more than give pious expression to general sentiments unless the public is willing to build up the national military strength to a point where general disapproval can make itself specifically felt. But few democracies are willing to pay the price necessary to make their internationalism constructive. Few are willing to examine the specific steps which are necessary to initiate a policy which would endeavor to remove the causes of war, because every specific policy requires readjustment of specific interests represented by specific pressure groups in close touch with their Congressmen and vocal before the country at large. It is inconsistent of the American public to endorse a policy of exaction of war debts payment simultaneously with a policy of high tariffs, but it is inconvenient to abandon either. It is inconsistent to condemn conquest while refusing to cooperate to prevent it, but both the condemnation and the nonco-operation are cherished American symbols that meet with ready response. In advance of a crisis, therefore, democratic governments are likely to take no more effective action than that exemplified by the Kellogg Pact, which outlawed

war only to the extent of causing belligcrents to
omit its declaration.

While the democracies are thus drifting, the
way of dictatorship is being blazed across the map.
Through incident after incident, the world is con-
fronted with the choice of accepting a Fascist
peace or entering a new general controversy. In
the course of the 1930's the dictatorships have
built up tremendous military power and shown
an increasing capacity for taking risks and carrying through coups d'état which democratic governments cannot take and carry through as long
as they remain democratic. In case of war, the dictatorships have in that capacity an unquestioned
initial advantage. It remains to be seen whether
their advantage in that respect is outbalanced by
certain advantages of the democracies. The claim
is made that already the dictatorships have so
keyed up their people and mobilized their countries that their strength is now at a maximum,
whereas the democracies, living at lower tension,
have additional reserves. It is further claimed that
the democracies have a suppleness and a self-reli-
ance which in the regimented states has all but
disappeared. On the other hand, democratic public opinion which shrinks from the horrors of immediate war may put its government in the position of acceding to a subsequent peace on terms
not of its choosing.

The way of dictatorship is a way which various peoples of the world have taken because of the inadequacy of their previous institutions, economic and political. Recent economic failures have been common property of the industrialized nations; in the failures of the political institutions of the past generation, the democracies, as the makers and former enforcers of the Treaty of Versailles, have a full share of responsibility to shoulder. Recognition of the causes of the way of dictatorship is important to those who turn from it to study the way of democracy.

CHAPTER IV

THE WAY OF DEMOCRACY

The way of democracy may be approached from various starting points. Some attempts at definition place their chief emphasis upon certain goals, with the inference that society becomes democratic as these goals are attained. The concept of democracy as the achievement of certain goals has become increasingly popular as the concern of the state with the economic process has increased. Rising standards of living are looked upon as the gradual democratization of property; the democratic state and the welfare state are seen as one.

Clearly, the attainment of a measure of economic security by its citizens is a goal of the contemporary democratic state; but equally clearly, that goal or any other is insufficient to distinguish it as democratic. The partial character of the goal theory of democracy can be demonstrated by reviewing the public statements of the leaders of the dictatorships, who number efficiency and material progress among their primary goals, and boast of them as totalitarian achievements.

For this reason, other attempts to define de-

mocracy stress the fact that since an identical outward result may be arrived at by means which
are paternalistic or despotic as well as by means
which are democratic, democracy should be defined not in terms of ends but in terms of means.
According to such views, the heart of the difference between the democracies and the totalitarian
states lies in their respective methods of defining
and serving the general welfare. In a democracy
effort will continually be made to debate the nature of the general welfare and to debate the
methods of serving the general welfare. In a totalitarian state the general welfare is defined by one
man or a rather small group of men without con-
sultation with the people, and defined in terms of
the glorification of one man or one group of men
or one race or one nation. The theories of democracy which define it as a means are correspondingly concerned with the methods, the governmental techniques, by which democracies ascer-
tain and carry on the people's business.

Closer to the whole truth are the definitions
which look upon national life as a corporate journey and democracy as a way of organizing for the
journey. Both goals and methods change with the
topography at various states of the march. But the
society can remain consistently democratic in giving its individuals maximum opportunity for development and self-expression on the one hand,

and for co-operation and self-organization on the other. Democracy thus becomes broader than a system of government; it becomes a way of life.

Democracy as a way of life may be characterized as including:

First, action based on the will of the majority after the people have had opportunity to inform themselves as to the real facts.

Second, freedom of speech, press, art, science and religion.

Third, stability, order and the avoidance of violence, bloodshed and anarchy.

Fourth, promotion of a stable but ascending general welfare by increasing the productivity of the people and by adopting price, wage and other policies which distribute income more evenly among the people but which do not diminish the incentive to increase production. This means continuous co-ordination of policies and functions.

Fifth, belief that there are extraordinary possibilities in both man and nature which have not yet been realized, but which can be made manifest only if the individualistic yet co-operative genius of democratic institutions is preserved, thus making it possible for those who are gifted in art, science and religion to approach the unknown reverentially, and not under the compulsion of producing immediate results for the glorification of one man, one group, one race or one nation.

Sixth, joyous faith in a progressive future based on the intelligent and constructive efforts of all the people to serve the general welfare.

Seventh, tolerance and humor which in recognizing the right of all men to be different, smiles understandingly at those who are so different as to be funny.

The struggles of the past one hundred and fifty years in the democratic countries may be interpreted as efforts to create the proper institutions for the expression of this way of life; to create a social structure which can contain and give will and determination to the democratic state of mind.

At the end of the eighteenth century, when the democratic ideas which for some generations had stirred in the minds of men first began to be expressed in terms of institutions, society was structurally extremely rigid. Its customs, its ideas and its system were concerned primarily with privilege and prerogative. The democrats of that time demanded a fundamental change in the functions of governments and ruling classes, and once they had stated their general objectives they had to go down into the political arena and formulate a program; they had to show what actual steps should be taken in order that government might exist for the benefit of free and equal citizens united in a common purpose, the happiness of each and all.

Brief reference to the evolution of British institutions illustrates this process. England took at least half of the sixteenth century to achieve a national church independent of the Pope. She took almost the whole of the seventeenth century for the more difficult task of setting up a constitutional monarchy controlled by a strong oligarchy; in other words, to change from a government mainly monarchial to a government by the classes that had recently got knowledge and with it power. And England found herself in the nineteenth and still finds herself in the twentieth century in the stream of a revolution roughly analogous to that of the seventeenth, for now much larger classes have got knowledge, and with it power, and the problem is once again to adapt English institutions to the uses of vast numbers who demand and who should have a part in public affairs.

The British system reposes ultimately upon two simple concepts, that the Government must govern and that the Opposition must criticize. The British have effected the union, the de facto union, of the executive and legislative arms of government. All executive power is exerted in the name of the King, but it is actually exerted by a group of about twenty ministers who are the leaders of the party in majority control of the elected branch of Parliament, the House of Commons. The Gov ernment then must govern and the Opposition must criticize, the forum of criticism being the Parliament, the microphone of criticism being the press, the audience being the people as a whole. Innately, essentially, this is a strictly democratic form of government. It may be charged that the party in power, using its majority, may pass objectionable legislation, to which the answer is that if the objectionableness of the legislation becomes intolerable, the criticism of the Opposition eventually has sufficient weight to cause the overturn of the Government and bring the Opposition into power.

The transformation in the exercise of executive power which has made the current form of British Government possible was a result of the relationship between George the Third and his Parliament, a relationship so objectionable to certain Englishmen living in England that some of the most brilliant victories of the American War of Independence were won on the floor of the British House of Commons by men like Chatham, Burke and Fox. Out of that conflict emerged a governmental system whose secret of efficiency is that the executive and legislative powers are one.

The American contemporaries of the British statesmen who effected this unification were too close to the event for its significance to be clearly perceived. Moreover, their primary problems lay in another field. General Washington, newly sworn in as President of the United States, said, "I walk on untrodden ground," and that was profoundly true. Everything was to be done. The executive structure which had replaced the Continental Congress consisted of little more than a Department of Foreign Affairs with hardly a dispatch to write, a Treasury whose chief contents were abundant evidences of domestic and foreign debt, and a corporal's guard of an army. And the new state had to be modeled upon a Constitution whose power to endure was gravely doubted by such men as Hamilton, Madison and others who had made it.

An English historian once described the United States of that time as a great ship, undermanned and poorly equipped. The duty of the average country elsewhere was to furnish as well as it could the government for the people living within its borders. The immediate duty of the United States was to find people to settle the land and capital to put them to work. Out of this need came the succession of land policies which for generations opened new areas to new immigrants; came the series of decisions of Chief Justice John Marshall which set the tone of the Constitutional canon for a great many years to come; came eventually a development which led an American historian of eminence to say that to a degree un-

known in any other country the social and political system of the United States is based upon industrial property right. The very heart of the system was industrial freeholding, and that was so
because it had to be so if the development, in a
century and a half, of the resources of the continental areas of the United States was to be
achieved. And accompanying the process of fever-
ish development was a looseness in banking systems, in the application of the limited liability
and joint-stock idea for capital development, and
in a hundred other manifestations which consti-
tuted, if considered generally, an acceptance of
wide risks in order that the business of building
a nation should go on. The economic power thus
generated became the lever for political changes.

The gentlemen who assembled in Philadelphia
did not frame the Constitution to set up what
would now be called a democracy. They framed
it with a shrewd awareness of the property basis
of political power, and a lively fear of what were
called leveling doctrines or doctrines of the masses.
The document as framed was a remarkable
achievement in the avoidance of majority rule.
To the people was given only the House of Representatives. The presidency was removed as far
from popular vote as it could be placed, that is to
say, it was transferred to an electoral college which
was supposed to use its independent judgment in

the choice of a president. The Senate, as James Madison remarked one day during the Constitutional Convention, was to be a body "whose limited number, and firmness might seasonably interpose against impetuous councils"; and the device selected to secure this end was election by the legislatures of the various States.

The first move away from this system was the capture of the presidency by the people through the inauguration of the party system. The people then had in their power both the House of Representatives and the presidency. The death, on July 4, 1826, of both Adams and Jefferson closed a period in American life. With the coming in of Andrew Jackson the United States became more and more definitely a democracy, demanding and obtaining increased breadth of suffrage long before it was granted in England. The adaptation of American institutions to those who in larger number gathered knowledge and with it power then began its rapid course; and the presidency became increasingly the weapon by which the people found it possible to assert their sovereignty.

Finally, around 1890, the great key year in American modern history, the frontier ended. America began to take on a new complexion almost at once. The demand for Constitutional amendment grew. There had been many demands for Constitutional amendment since 1804, but

until 1913 there had been no amendments save
the three which were born of the agony and tra-
vail of the Civil War. But in 1913 two amendments were ratified.

One of them decreed the popular election of
Senators. Through that amendment the people,
who in the beginning had been given the House
of Representatives and had later acquired control
over the presidency through the operation of the
party system, rounded out their power over the
executive and legislative arms of the government.

The other amendment of 1913 permitted the
imposition of a graduated Federal income tax to
be laid without apportionment among the States.
The importance of the income tax amendment
was this: when the income tax was passed and
collected, and when the returns were made public, the American people for the first time in their
national history had a picture, a design in the
form of figures, showing the amount and manner
of distribution of American wealth. In other
words, the people that had just rounded out their
control over the executive and legislative arms of
the government through the senatorial amendment were given a mark to shoot at. The American people have been shooting at it ever since and
are continuing to shoot. Officially, theoretically,
ideally, the powers of government in the United
States are divided into executive, legislative and

judicial. But behind that official distribution of power there lies an ultimate reality. The real division of power in the United States has long been between the voters and the property holders, the voters, in ultimate and effective control of the executive and legislative arms of the government, as over against the property holders, with the Supreme Court sitting as arbiter between them.

Walter Bagehot in his "Physics and Politics" said that society in its early form creates a large area of reflex action, a "cake of custom," and thereby achieves stability; but that as time goes on society must break upward through that cake of custom in order to achieve progress. Now the cake of custom created by the United States was made of industrial property right; it facilitated growth and over a long period provided stability. But a break upward through that cake of custom now appears necessary, in order to establish, through the process known as social legislation, public equities in what has hitherto been considered private property. The result is the issue between voters and property holders as it is today.

Developments related to this issue suggest that the United States is now approaching the problem which faced the British nation at the time of the American Revolution. The executive and the legislative are both under the control of the popular vote and yet they are, as they have been ever since

the days of General Washington, generally in conflict. The difficulty of throwing a bridge between
the executive and the legislative appears to be
both real and permanent, particularly because of
the Constitutional provision which maintains du-
ality between the two. An effective bridge of communication between them might be anticipated in
the bridge of party. But the party has been an insufficient and uncertain bridge, largely for the
reason that the Federal system hamstrings the
party system. American parties must act with a
view to controlling not only the national government, but the governments of forty-eight states.
In striving to be all things to all states they therefore tend to resort to patronage and spoils as more
effective means of achieving unity than policy
based on principle. The result is to weaken the
party as a bridge between executive and legislative, a bridge greatly needed if there is to be any
such coherence in the performance of governmental functions as wise men would desire.

This difficulty of finding a bridge has con-
tributed in a very considerable measure to the
growth of the presidency as the only weapon by
which the people can assert their sovereignty. In
a large portion of its activities, Congress acts as a
regional, not a national, body. Most major legislation passed by the Congress of the United States
takes the form of treaties peacefully concluded be-

tween the great regions of the country. No state as a state has much power in Congress. Only groups of states can exert power there. News of a "farm bloc" is in fact news of a region at work within the Congressional body. To the extent that Congress is a regional body, the national ideal of the American people increasingly tends to find its embodiment, its incarnation, in the President of the United States. Political issues in this country are rarely made by Congress; they are made by the President of the United States. A list of successful presidents is a list of men who served not only as chief executive but as chief legislator; they were chief executives who were able to secure passage of their legislative programs by that regional body, the Congress of the United States.

The strengthening of the executive seems a tendency which is wholly likely to go on, especially if it is recognized that no Congress as it is in the United States, no Parliament as it is in England, is capable of the initiatory stage of legislation for the simple reason that it does not have the information required. Wise use of the initiatory power by the executive is, however, conditioned by two necessities, the availability of an alert civil service, and the functioning of an active opposition.

It was Benjamin Disraeli who first said that the most important adjunct of any government is a vigorous opposition, and subsequent experience

has shown that its lack is possibly the greatest liability that a government can suffer. Recognition
of the duty of the executive to recommend legislation must therefore be paralleled by recognition
of the duty of Congress to criticize.

A similar understanding of the proper functioning of the civil service is equally necessary in
a system which is to see an extension of the executive power as the chief weapon in the hands of the
people for the achievement of their ends. The civil
service is the treasure house of administrative experience and competence, and its importance increases as the application of science to life compli-
cates the problem of government. The function
of the civil service is to make available to the
political arm facts, experience and judgments relative to the program which the executive is prepared to propose. In providing these it must respect the demarcation between the political and
administrative functions—it must not itself pre-
sume after political power. The duty of the civil
service is to make its opinion heard, but not its
will prevail.

The importance of the adequate fulfillment of
these three functions, government, opposition, administration, is all the more necessary in view of
the current transition from the legal state of the
nineteenth century to the welfare state of the
twentieth. John J. Chapman once wrote that most

government in the United States is an incident in
the history of commerce, a part of the triumph of
industrial progress. In order to make such a reference true of Great Britain, it would be necessary
to say that most government in Great Britain has
been successively an incident in the development
of the monarchy, the barony, the church, and finally, in the present, an incident in the history
of commerce, a part of the triumph of industrial
progress. For Chapman's dictum is no less true
for Great Britain because the force of tradition,
the force of usage, and the corporate nature of
much of its life has not permitted business, industry and commerce to occupy so overwhelming a
share of the national interest as it does in the
United States. All modern governments are assert-
ing, because of the need to assert it, an ever
greater control over the economic process. This
has been more difficult in the United States than
in Great Britain because of the existence of a written constitution and because the canon of judicial
interpretation over a considerable period was
highly unfavorable to any disturbance of the idea
that property was antecedent to government and
should be put beyond the reach of majorities. In
the nineteenth century the state was something
which could be described as a legal state. The general idea under which the democracies operated
was that if each man pursued his own interest

the totality of these individual interests would by
some process coincide with the general or common interest. It did not take very long for the
fallacy of this idea to be manifest in many minds
and laissez-faire suffered progressive losses in public esteem. But while laissez-faire continued, the
duty of the state was to see that the interest of the
people as a whole should not be harmful to property. It now appears that the state of the twentieth
century is and will increasingly become a welfare
state. There is nothing undemocratic in this. It
does not establish any growth of authority over
liberty beyond what should be. It does not strike
at the base of representative government. It is a
fact. Indeed it is a fact so universally admitted
that it is the very heart and center not only of the
system of the democracies but the justification of
Fascism, of Nazism and of Communism. Each one
of those systems asserts that it is based upon social
welfare, the welfare of all. In this respect, the current competition between systems is not so much
competition in ideologies as competition in how
best to provide for the general welfare. The democracies believe that the state should be the
agent of the nation. The dictatorships believe that
the nation is the creature of the state. The United
States, along with other democratic states, must
rely for endurance in its present form on its ability
to adapt its institutions to a period of change

more rapid than any that has preceded it, and it is clear that further changes are impending. In the United States as in Great Britain an enlargement of the area of democratic action is in process, with the people laying hold of first the executive and legislative, and finally the judicial power as the ultimate agency of their will.

The problems of the coming period are the problems which Madison foresaw. Capitalism, if given free rein, destroys democracy. The "wealthy and wellborn," if allowed to go their way without check generation after generation, lose touch with the soil, lose touch with the great body of the people; and in losing touch with the way life is actually lived by the bulk of the people, they inevitably destroy democracy. On the other hand, democracy requires a discipline that is increasingly rigorous as economic conditions become more complex.

Modern democracy requires a high degree of economic literacy among its citizens. In a pioneer civilization, democracy had less need to concern itself about budgetary and monetary policy or how the expenditure policies of the government affect the production of goods from year to year. Grave errors were committed with respect to these problems, but a frontier society could compensate for its errors by opening more of the abundant cheap land to the west. Today these problems are inescapable.

Cool heads are needed to meet them. In the organizing period of the welfare state it is easy for demagogues to thrive on political confusion, to cause farmers to believe that they can obtain by fiat two dollars a bushel for wheat, twenty cents a pound for cotton, a dollar a bushel for corn, thirty cents a pound for tobacco and fifteen dollars a hundred for hogs, and to cause labor to believe that it can increase wages and cut hours indefinitely. At the same time it is equally possible for plutogogues to cause businessmen to believe that they are entitled to increase their profits and reduce their taxes indefinitely. Such economic illiteracy threatens democracy simultaneously from the right and from the left.

It is possible to run a middle-of-the-road modern democracy in competition with the modern totalitarian states only to the extent that its citizens are willing to accept a discipline of the general welfare; and at the moment there is equal need of preaching that discipline in the United States among the bottom third and among the top five percent. The essential of the democracy of the future is an attitude of tolerant co-operation, giving play to the common sense by which a policy for commonwealth can be created.

In a democracy, it is improbable that the discipline of co-operative policy-making can be nationally instilled. It must be a local product. A democratic society is the kind of society in which policy slowly and uncertainly and hesitatingly emerges out of thousands of conferences and millions of conversations, out of pressure groups, out of the opinion of the press, and out of all the paraphernalia that a free country employs to make vocal the opinion of its citizens. A country in which that kind of discussion goes on is in direct contrast to the kind of society in which policy is superimposed from above.

The week after the occupation of Austria, Hitler is reported to have said: "On Friday night I was not even thinking of Austria—then suddenly I knew that the deed and the hour was predetermined in history. I did not make the decision—it came to me. I did not consult anyone. I gave the orders." Now in states where policy-making takes this form, the orders given not infrequently do express the desires and interests of a very large percentage of the population. Not infrequently the dictators, by all the chicanery of which they are capable through press and radio and propaganda service, can prepare a people so that a majority of the people does desire the orders when they are given. But whether or not there is popular approval of the final decision, the process of

making the decision is clearly the negation of democracy.

The unique contribution of democracy to the
world has been the representative system of government, a system of government through which
the varied and diverse interests, opinions, likes,
dislikes, preferences and prejudices of the citizens
can become articulate in the body politic. Something like a Parliament or a Congress is essential
to democratic institutions. The Prime Minister in
Great Britain, the President in the United States,
may be looked upon as the representative-in-chief
of the people. But no one man can in his own
mind and spirit represent a continent of 120 million people with its myriad life, its various sections, regions, races, organizations. Nor has one
man the capacity for self-criticism, for the expression of His Majesty's Opposition, that is abso-
lutely essential in a democratic society. Only
through a representative body can the vital variety of democratic society be reflected.

Descriptions of the functioning of the representative process usually emphasize two stages: the
election of the representatives and the meeting at
which the elected assemble to make policy. But
the heart of the representative process lies elsewhere: it lies in the citizens to whom the elections
offer an opportunity to select representatives. The
agenda of Congress is not made upon the floor of

the Senate or the House. It is made by the citizens
and groups of citizens whose desires are communi-
cated to their representatives and acted on in proportion to urgency and pressure.

In a democracy there is a due process of policy-
making no less than a due process of law. Due
process of policy-making occurs in those communities where a perennial argument about national
policy is carried on among responsible citizens
representing a cross section of the community's
life, an argument begun with facts and reliable
opinion about them, and carried forward until generally acceptable conclusions have been
reached. These citizens are the men and women
who make the opinion of their various communities. They are a voluntary group, not an organ
of government, and not so large a number as the
electorate; responsible persons concerned about
the public welfare, and thinking in terms of the
interest of the community and of the part of the
community which they represent as labor leaders,
farm leaders, factory managers, professional men.

Due process of policy-making is more important
than elections—Hitler was elected in Germany. It
is even more important than the deliberations of
Congress because it gives Congress something to
deliberate about: if the representative assembly
is to be wise in its formulation of national policy,
there must be a local soil out of which national

policy can grow. Evidences of erosion have been ominously frequent in the public policy of the United States for the past seventy-five years. It is common knowledge that there are relatively few groups functioning locally to whose deliberations the above description of the due process of policy-making can be applied. The need for a soil conservation program in this field is patent.

There are two related reasons why these groups should be so few, why the country should have suffered from such a long depression in the intelligent concern of responsible citizens about the policy of their national government.

The political default of the American middle classes is closely related to the exploitation of the continent. From the Civil War to the World War the middle class of America had its mind on business to the exclusion of almost everything else. After generations of free popular education, when colleges far to the west of the Atlantic seaboard were preparing for their centenaries, the majority of their graduates was placing its chief reliance for intellectual stimulus on the speakers at its luncheon clubs. Social prestige was based so exclusively on economic success that no considerable number of members of the middle-class group—the group that has been the mainstay of every democracy—was vitally concerned with the general welfare of the society in which it lived. The middle class was

so busy with its profits that it forfeited its role as
maker of an intelligent and sound national policy.

The economic overemphasis of recent generations, moreover, has accentuated a trend toward
functional sectionalism which has become a
further obstacle to the due process of policy-making. The country has already suffered one experience of the disruptiveness of an overemphasized
sectionalism, the geographic sectionalism that led
to the War between the States. The roots of the
current form of sectionalism go far back into the
American past. The manufacturing sector dates
back at least to the Tariff of Abominations of
1828: some people would begin it with Hamilton. The labor sector and the farm sector came
much later, but all of these sectors, and smaller
ones of the various professional people, are organized and active today.

In the thousands of localities which form the
constituencies of the country, these different functional and occupational groups meet separately.
Such meetings are indispensable, in order that
the members of the group may have an informed
understanding of their group interest and a policy
for its furtherance. But the very success of their
separate discussions may endanger the process of
general policy-making unless there is local consul-
tation, local cross-fertilization among the groups,
going on at the same time as their functional ac-

tivities. The tendency now is toward national federation of the local groups of each kind, toward the formation of pressure groups which move on Washington in blocs demanding that their interests be advanced. Congress and the President thus become practically the sole source of whatever concept of the general welfare receives attention. So far as the constituencies are concerned, the representative system becomes representation of special interests.

The fault in the system is thus a local, not a national, fault. If sound democratic policy is to be made, it must be initiated in local discussions participated in by leaders of farm, industrial, labor and professional groups in their home towns. Where such discussion takes place, the give-and-take, the bargain, the compromise that is the characteristic mark of democracy, is continually going on in local arguments, local conversations. The process of moderation is continually minimizing what appear to be irreconcilable differences in interest. Where such discussion takes place, representatives in Congress have a concept of the general welfare to represent.

The true interests of the farm group in America can never be adequately cared for if agriculture approaches the national government solely as a functional bloc. The farm group alone in an industrial nation can never dominate the scene. It has to work in alliance, to learn to give and take with other groups. And that process of coming in touch with other groups, of working out policies with other groups, of moderating particular demands in the light of the larger community, should begin locally in order that when farm policy reaches the national stage it may be a reasoned presentation instead of an emotional demand which cannot be reconciled with similar emotional demands of other interests.

When the responsible middle class allows its political function to go by the board, and exploits or leaves untended the social soil which the democratic process requires for its sustenance, two results are likely to follow. Political weeds replace soundly rooted policies in the eroded localities. And the economic floods which local erosion permits to gather cause the national government to undertake the making of policy as a measure of public works.

To the extent that the representative system, through the default of the middle class in its constituencies, arrives at a point where the representative has only a vacuum, an emotion or a special interest to represent, national policy-making will be increasingly done by the executive with the advice of his experts. The experts tend to be men who have never been subject to the discipline of local election, and such local and even Congressional policy-making as they have seen done in the name of democracy may have given them contempt for the process. Their interest is thus inclined to be in goals for democracy rather than in methods of democracy. An executive program made in such a mood is in constant danger of crossing the line from being government by, to becoming government for, the people.

The unique institution of democracy is the representative assembly. Dictatorships have executives. Dictatorships have supreme courts. But dictatorships do not have representative assemblies with the right to give legal recognition to the policies of the people. The due process of policy-making, whereby public opinion is evolved out of a continuous give-and-take in communities, counties, states and nation, puts the elected officers of the republic in a position to declare a genuine national policy. It is the indispensable characteristic of the way of democracy.

CHAPTER V

INSTRUMENTS OF POLICY-MAKING

THE instruments by which public opinion is converted into public procedure need to be continually re-examined with an eye to the impact of scientific innovations. The application of science to social ends may cause social behavior to differ so materially from the social behavior of the period when existing governmental techniques were established that the techniques lose most of their pertinence. The resulting need for review then runs all the way from the provisions for freedom of speech, press, religion and assembly on the part of the individual citizens, through the mechanics of the various semi-public agencies and organizations making proposals for public policy, to the activities of the government bodies that turn political policy into public procedure. People who are interested in the contemporary mechanics of the democratic process are particularly likely to give attention to these problems because of their appreciation that applied science has introduced a precision into the social process, particularly the economic process, which requires a corresponding precision in the mechanics by which it is guided and controlled.

New techniques in printing, and new inventions in radio and motion pictures have altered beyond recognition the conditions of individual freedom current when the Declaration of Rights announced freedom of speech and of the press. Freedom of speech was then affirmed as subject to no limitation except the law of libel. But the Declaration of Rights tacitly assumed that free speech was physically limited by the restricted range of a man's unaided voice. Science has since removed that restriction: radio, sound films, amplifiers, electrical recordings have pushed out the limits of time and space to which freedom of speech was formerly subject. Today what is one voice against a loud speaker?

Now no less than yesterday there are physical limits to the transmission of ideas, but they are very different limits from the limits assumed by the framers of the Bill of Rights. The new inventions mean wider mass distribution from increasingly centralized sources. Radio transmission is confined to a certain number of wave lengths, and possible only to stations of a certain strength. It is estimated that there are some nine and a half million radios tuning in day by day from the rural areas of the United States. Movie attendance in the villages and county seats within easy driving distance of farms runs into the thousands every week. By what means, under today's technology, can the basic concepts of rural American culture be brought to the cities in a manner proportionate to the impact of city culture upon the farms? What instruments of control, what guarantees are necessary to freedom of speech under these new conditions?

Comparable changes have similarly affected freedom of the press. Until three generations ago, most newspapers were one-man shows, and freedom to print meant freedom of that one man to set his ideas up in type and circulate them. Today, only the rural weeklies conform to this picture. Today, newspapers, radio and movies are big business, employing thousands of people and requiring a capital outlay of hundreds of millions of dollars. Between forty and forty-five million newspapers roll off the presses of the United States every day; news broadcasts are at the dials of nearly thirty million radio sets; news reels are offered to a weekly motion picture attendance that runs from seventy to eighty million.

The present limits of distribution of news, ideas and beliefs are moreover likely to be pushed still further. The imminence of television is a matter of daily comment; in London, it has already arrived. Improvement in transmission of photographs by radio or telegraph has proceeded

at a rate during the last two or three years sufficient to justify a prediction that the method may
soon be extended to the whole paper. In that
case a newspaper could be printed in New York
and transmitted by telegraph to every large city
in the country for reproduction simultaneously
with the New York edition. Another experimental
mechanism enables one man at some central point
to sit at a keyboard and cause type to be set in a
thousand newspaper offices over the country. Already on the market is a radio printer, a fairly
inexpensive mechanism attachable to radio sets in
individual homes, to print newspapers between
twelve midnight and seven A.M. What of freedom
of the press under conditions such as these?

The freedom of the press which the Declaration of Rights guaranteed to the one-man newspaper was freedom from government censorship.
The methods then current for producing newspapers were assumed. Today, the mechanical
equipment necessary for the production of a modern paper requires so great a capital outlay that
a corporate urban interest is almost invariably
involved in the running of a paper. Conflict between the economic or ideological interest of the
publisher and the welfare of the community, at
some point or other, can be taken for granted.
The point will vary, depending on whether the
publisher is a big business corporation, a co-

operative, a trade union, or a political party; but at that point a filter will be put between the public and the news. The mechanical process of mass production of newspapers has thus been accompanied by a practice of private censorship quite as important as government censorship but concerning which the Bill of Rights makes no specifications.

Under conditions of current technology, freedom of the press, defined as the absence of censorship, appears to be Utopian. The choice may therefore be assumed to lie between private censorship by special interests and government censorship.

The practical solution to the problems of private censorship appears to lie not in the elimination of special interests, but in the generalization of sources of pressure to provide something more nearly equivalent to proportionate representation of the various interests of which the country is composed.

It takes eight to ten million dollars to start in the newspaper business in a city of any size, and gross earnings of ten to fifteen million dollars are not impossible. Overrepresentation of urban interests and overrepresentation of wealth are normal outgrowths of such conditions. The man—or more likely the group of men—who can muster the necessary money is apt to come from the same class in the community as the other big business men who run steel, or the railroads, or the bond or banking houses. In general, he has the same kind of ideas that they have, and that the firms which give his paper its advertising have; and he wants to make money with his paper. Yet the resulting distortion of the news is less great than might be anticipated from these circumstances.

The news columns of many papers publish fairly complete and unbiased accounts of events. Two forces are at work to this end. One is the attitude of the working newspaperman who views the newspaper essentially as a carrier which delivers his goods to the public, and who is prepared to fight for free carriage. But the big newspapers of today are built up out of too many individual decisions for highly personalized control to be practicable: hence the other major force toward unbiased reporting is the development of news-gathering agencies like the Associated Press, the United Press, the International News Service and others, whose simultaneous clients range all the way from left to right. The reader who has access to these dispatches is in a fairly good position to draw his own conclusions as to the policy which contemporary events make desirable; when the editor of the paper is bludgeoned with the blue pencil of special interest, the reader can vote for the news columns as against the editorial page.

Moreover, a direct competitor of the editorial page has appeared with the rise of the syndicated column as a newspaper institution. As newspaper production shifted from the one-man office to the big industrial plant, public recognition of private censorship was reflected in the loss of prestige and influence of the editorial page. Public interest in independent opinion is reflected in the current popularity of the commentators whose syndicated articles are free from the brass check of the particular journals in which they appear.

The plurality of sources of both news and views available to American readers under the current system of private censorship thus affords a considerable measure of freedom of the press, even though corporate representation of the left is rare in the publishing business. Under such a system, however, the final safeguard must necessarily be the critical sense of the reader, his capacity to recognize coloring in the news, and to consider occasional demands on the editorial page and occasional silences in the news columns in the light of the special interests of particular papers as private enterprises.

If the private censorship characteristic of today's American press was unforeseen when the Declaration of Rights listed freedom of the press

among the fundamental civil liberties, likewise
unforeseen was the type of government dictation
of the news which is the increasingly prevalent
alternative.

Clearly, if the press is not to be a private enterprise it must be a government organ, either under
government operation or under government control or under a voluntary form of government
censorship. Classification of the countries of the
world according to the degree of current government interference with freedom of speech and of
the press yields the following results:

The countries where there is no freedom of
any kind, where the government has control over
press, radio, motion pictures, classroom and pul-
pit, are the countries in which about two-thirds
of the world's population—roughly 1,350,000,000
people—live. In a second group of countries there
is a fluctuating degree of freedom of speech and
thought. When no serious tension is being felt
in these countries, when nothing in particular is
going on, a considerable degree of freedom is
available; when tension increases, freedom correspondingly contracts. About two-ninths of the
world's population—roughly 450,000,000 people
—have this fluctuating degree of freedom. The
citizens of the third group of countries enjoy approximately as much freedom as there is in the
United States. Only about one-ninth of the

world's population—some 225,000,000 people—is in this group.

The extent to which the press of the dictatorship countries is regimented can be gathered from the weekly instructions to editors giving government orders as to what shall be played up, what shall be played down, what words shall and shall not be used. It is true that newspaper circulation falls off under a dictatorship as people realize that all the papers are the same, but the fact remains that only one version of events is in circulation. Readers with a high critical sense may use their papers to see what the government has ordered circulated, and deduce from that what is giving the government anxiety, and deduce from that what is going on. But for the less critical reader, and particularly for the nation's youth, exposure to only one source of ideas is likely to end in indoctrination and atrophy of the critical sense.

The totalitarian relationship between government and press, moreover, cannot be dismissed merely as an undesirable foreign alternative to the American system as currently operated. In all countries, including the United States, the increased participation of the government in the economic process, the inauguration of nation-wide programs affecting agriculture, business and finance, has materially changed the relationship between the government and the news. Information on government activities is now a primary objective of news-gathering agencies, and the channels for making this news available represent a relationship unforeseen when the Declaration of Rights guaranteed a hands-off attitude to the press on the part of the government.

The current contacts of government with press and radio are matters of great interest to those concerned with the functioning of democracy. If newspapermen are to perform their function of getting news of the government through their papers to the public they must have proper access to sources of information.

In recent years, government information given to the press has been increasingly canalized by the establishment of information services attached to the various government departments, often with former newspapermen in charge. Big business has for some time been in the habit of appointing Vice-Presidents in Charge of Public Relations, with the function of securing a good press for the corporation, and, on occasion, of soft-pedaling hot news. Government information services organized on that model would render a disservice to democracy. It is the job of the newspapermen covering a government department to convey not only the facts as to what is going on, but the outlines of the reasoning on which action is being based. Otherwise the public is not in a position to make a genuine choice between alternative policies. Knowledge of the motives and objectives which have led public officials to take certain steps is necessary to an intelligent evaluation of long-term policies, and to the making of democratic choices between divergent paths. In a democracy it is therefore the job of the government information services not only to supply the press with announcements of current operations, with statistics, and with the speeches, statements of policy, etc., of the ranking group of departmental officers, but to put reporters and others seeking information in touch with the persons, offices and publications related to the problem at hand, so that independent interpretations of national policy, based upon firsthand contact, are continually available to the people whose judgment is expressed at the polls.

Freedom of the press is usually urged on the ground that without it, public opinion lacks an adequate basis of fact. An informed electorate is cited as the mainspring of democratic action. The Constitution makers based their faith in democracy on the capacity of the individual citizen to exercise rational choice.

But the Constitution makers lived before the days of political machines. Persons interested in more recent political behavior must consider de-

scriptions such as that which Ostrogorski made at
the opening of this century: "If on the map of
the United States all the parts of the country
where the Machine has developed were coloured
red, the eye would at once be attracted to the
right by a large blotch formed by the States of
New York and Pennsylvania with a strip of the
State of New Jersey on the east, with the State
of Maryland on the south, and the State of Ohio
on the west. This spot casts a faint shadow to the
north-east over New England, while on the other
side, to the west, the red will appear in more or
less deep tints on the State of Illinois, and will
stain the neighbouring States, marking with scarlet points most of the large cities, such as St. Louis
in Missouri and others of less importance, like
Louisville in Kentucky or Minneapolis in Minne-
sota, and other still smaller ones among the large
ones; then, after making a brief pause in the States
of the Far West and leaving some patches there,
it will flow toward the Pacific slope and deposit
a thick layer of carmine on San Francisco; and,
finally, jumping right over to the Gulf of Mexico,
it will cover New Orleans with a similar layer.
A very considerable space will be left hardly coloured at all or will even exhibit the shot colour
to be seen in certain fabrics: these are regions or
cities where the Machine has no stable and regular existence; rings of mercenary politicians form

in them, disappear after a short time, and re-form under favourable circumstances. A good many points again on the map will appear almost white, presenting the touching spectacle of 'good Machines.' . . . In any event, it must not be forgotten that the part of the map coloured red, while only a portion of the whole country, contains almost a third of the population of the United States and represents at least three-fifths of its economic interests."

Today's map would show that some of this scarlet has been whitewashed, and some of it genuinely cleaned up. Certain machines are however in as good working order as when Lincoln Steffens' "Shame of the Cities" was making news. But not only is this true today in the cities: there are machines in rural areas equally dependable in their operation if somewhat less rewarding in their output. Why have these machines flourished? Why are they an accepted method of doing public business in the American democracy?

Speaking from the center of Tammany experience, a master of Manhattan gave one reason: "It's because there's a mayor and a council and judges and a hundred other men to deal with. You can't do business with a lot of officials who check and cross one another and who come and go, in this year, out the next. A business man wants to do business with one man and one who is always there to remember and carry out the business."

If one reason for the boss and the machine is to give continuity and centralized direction to a complicated government agency, another is to act as an employment service to staff that agency. With a hundred years of practical experience behind it, including experience in how to handle situations technically designated as Civil Service, and more jobs than ever to fill, operation of the system of spoils and patronage remains a rewarding activity for political organizations.

A third reason for machine activity, at least until very recent years, has arisen from the absence of a wide social welfare program. What should have been provided the people as citizens has been given them by the machines as favors and matters of preference, with the understanding that they should drop their thanks into the ballot box. As one boss said, "I feed 'em, and, by God, I vote 'em."

The existence of an economic vacuum is what has made one of the major machine activities possible; but the existence of a political vacuum is what has made possible the whole phenomenon of the machine.

In a representative democracy, particularly one which attempts to operate on a continental scale, some bridge between the citizen and his government is clearly necessary. When the great bulk of average citizens, the middle class, is performing its proper function of policy-making, that bridge is normally the political party.

In the United States, political parties exist, and for long have largely existed, to win elections, not to discuss public policy. Between elections, the major parties practically go out of existence, leaving policy-making to pressure groups, and administration to machine-picked personnel. There is truth in the statement: "We have two political parties in this country, not because there are two sides to every question but because there are two sides to every office, outside and inside." Getting out the vote has so monopolized the attention of American party leaders and party organizations that the formulation of public policy has been left largely to chance and last-minute compromise. American parties have not organized themselves for consideration of national policy, have not attempted to develop machinery which would clear the air of platitudinous demagoguery and lead to general agreement among their adherents as to objectives and procedures. Undoubtedly, the task of getting agreement in a country as large and complex as the United States is very difficult, but it is comparably important for a healthy democracy.

British developments during the past hundred years—during, that is to say, the period in which

the spoils system has operated in the United States
—provide a record of successive steps away from
a comparable condition. The British Civil Service dates only from the latter half of the nineteenth century; prior to that time there was an
official dispenser of patronage attached to the
Treasury. The struggle for appointments between
the executive and the legislative—between King
and Parliament—at the end of the eighteenth and
beginning of the nineteenth century, particularly
over the positions and emoluments controlled by
the East India Company, is accurately enough
portrayed in Thackeray's "Vanity Fair." The Report of the Royal Commission appointed to in-
vestigate existing abuses, which recommended
competitive examination for entrance to the Civil
Service, was pronounced on its appearance to be
of a stern morality which the country would never
bear. But in the less than seventy years since Glad-
stone's administration established the British
Civil Service, patronage has been replaced by a
career service of nonpartisan efficiency.

Developments in policy-making have paralleled
those in administration. British parties have provided regular means of discussing and formulat-
ing party policy. Party conferences are held each
year at which programs of action are worked out.
If differences between leadership and rank and
file cannot be resolved, changes in leadership are

made until the party is able to maintain a certain discipline and present a reasonably united front; and at the same time cabinet ministers and party leaders are kept informed as to what their followers desire in a given situation.

In practically all of these aspects, British parties contrast with American. The quadrennial conferences of American parties give little time and less attention to the formulation of the party platforms, which are generally recognized as subject to change without notice following the election for which they aim to be vote-catchers. Prominent men in the same party may hold diametrically opposite views; usually the Chairman of the National Committee speaks only in his individual capacity; Congressional leadership is by seniority rather than in accordance with any plan of party structure and is functionally separated from executive leadership by Constitutional provision.

Perhaps the greatest contrast between British and American party procedure is that in the United States the party out of power feels small responsibility for providing the current administration with a persistent and coherent opposition, for maintaining the give-and-take of argument which is the foundation of democratic policy.

In making a comparison between the British and American parties, however, one aspect of the

British system which has considerably simplified
the task of British parties should not be lost to
view: British governments do not hold office for
fixed terms. The possibility of a general election
is continually before them, serving as a stimulus
to day-to-day preparedness which is much more
difficult to maintain in a country where presidents
and Congressmen hold office for stated numbers
of years. Moreover, since British governments
resign on specific issues, a party membership prepared to exercise intelligent choice on specific
issues is a more definite asset to a British party
than to an American party whose members, by
contrast, go to the polls to express accumulated
approval of, or accumulated grievance at, all that
has been done over a period of two, four or six
years.

The difficulty of interpreting an election mandate in terms of specific desires on specific issues
is a major problem of American politics. It is one
of the forces which has given rise to the series
of current attempts to measure public opinion by
polling cross sections of the population. The close
correlation between the results of recent elections,
and the predictions of the results made by the
agencies which pay careful attention to the com-
position of the sample public that they poll, sug-
gests that the polls may come to parallel the

political parties as a second bridge between the citizen and his government.

Prerequisite to the accuracy of such polls is proper sampling. Income, age, sex, party, religion, urban or rural residence, geographic location, relief or nonrelief status, are all factors to be taken into account. Equally important is the form in which the questions asked are stated; accurate results cannot be obtained from questions worded so as to encourage a particular type of answer. But answers to unbiased questions given by a representative sample of the population may have significance along several lines.

They may serve as a postelection check on the victorious party's interpretation of its mandate. There have been various occasions in the years since the War when the policy of the incoming administration with regard to a particular issue —say the League of Nations or Prohibition—could well have been checked by a poll of public opinion made in the absence of election fervors.

A second postelection use of polls of public opinion is to test the impact of the national programs which the current administration puts into force. If, for instance, the Department of Agriculture inaugurates a program under legislation passed in the belief that it would be of benefit to farmers, and a public-opinion poll indicates areas where dissatisfaction with the program is considerable, investigation of the reasons for the dissatisfaction may be of definite help to the administration in supplying constructive criticism which can be incorporated into the program.

Polls can be similarly useful in building up an agenda of public business prior to elections, or to party declarations of policy. Taken on a sectional basis, they can aid the working out of the necessary accommodation among the various regions of the country.

They can also test public opinion on subjects surrounded by social tabu; a year prior to the program inaugurated through the Surgeon General's office, polls indicated an overwhelming majority in favor of measures to control syphilis.

The strength of pressure groups can likewise be gauged by means of polls. It has often enough been demonstrated that pressure groups with considerable funds at their disposal can dispense with large memberships. Public-opinion polls afford a means of checking on their assertions. If a pressure group announces that it represents labor's views, or the farmers' views, or the views of any other interest, a poll can test the accuracy of the claim. Party strategies can be similarly checked.

Polls thus give the politician a new index to the interests and beliefs of his constituency and perform part of the function which coherent political parties could exercise. Otherwise, the poli-

tician has but two sources of information on what
his constituents want. He has before him, constantly before him, what the pressure groups in
his district say is best for the country. The politician who votes against his party on a given issue
is often exhibiting not political independence but
economic dependence—his party ties are simply
weaker than his pressure group tie-ups. For other
information about his constituents the present-
day American politician must rely largely on his
native instinct, and adopt the guiding principle
of the Tammany boss who said that all he did
was to study human nature and act accordingly.
Such a situation tends to fix, as the prevailing
political type, the man whose chief attributes are
a friendly disposition and a good memory for
names.

But however helpful the polls of public opinion
are in showing the mind of the country on a given
issue, they obviously cannot do the work that
might be performed by coherent political parties.
Political clearance of individuals applying for
jobs is an ancient practice in the United States
which could well be succeeded by political clearance of ideas applying for place on the legislative
calendar. Such a procedure would have far-reaching effects. It would eliminate some of the dis-
advantages which result from representation on
the basis of fairly small geographic units; the indi-

vidual legislator would be less parochial in his
views, less bound by the particular industry or
occupation dominant in his district, more able
to take part in the formation of national policy.

Parties based upon broad social concepts would
increase the political participation of two groups
of citizens now largely outside the political process. Serious activity in the formation of national
policy would attract a type of political intelligence
which for some generations has not been available for public purposes. The development and
continuous use of expert committees on the technical aspects of the party's program would enable
the party to draw on abilities which under current conditions are monopolized by private enterprise. Local and regional discussions to bring the
party program before the rank and file for consideration would provide opportunities for the
political apprenticeship of future members of
party councils. The national executive committees
would take on new importance as the organs
which weld the advice of the advisory committees and the findings of the local and regional
party meetings into coherent general programs.

The attraction which coherent political parties
would have for the highly trained expert and administrative talents of the community would
moreover be paralleled by political participation
among the general mass of the electorate due to

the educational work of such parties. When polls of public opinion are taken, from ten to twenty percent of the persons polled normally fail to reply on the grounds that they don't know enough about the issue to have an opinion. On some issues the "don't know" vote runs as high as one in three. The dangers of such an electorate are obvious: a mass of political illiterates is a standing invitation to machine manipulation—and in moments of acute social crisis its political participation is likely to go beyond the exchange of a political quid for an economic quo.

In the absence of consistently functioning parties the American legislator stands practically alone as the broker whose job it is to bring special interests together and to harness the tides of popular emotion so that something useful can come of their energy. His task is to be a specialist in the general welfare, to create some working concept of the general welfare out of the innumerable special requests and specific demands which fill his office with undisciplined clamor. This is how one legislator sees his job:

"Much legislation, of course, is something that doesn't have to be done, but there come times when you can't postpone social action any longer. In that situation you almost invariably have the representatives of two groups coming together, with one saying, 'Now, we have to have this,' and

the other saying, 'No, you can't have that.' They
may be miles apart. After the first bluff they each
give in just a little, but then each declares he
won't give in any further. If you are a wise politician, you will postpone the decision if you can.

"But there are times when you can't put things
off, and then what are you going to do about it?
The representative of each group has wrapped its
economic interest, or professional or personal
pride, in what seems to him an impenetrable
blanket of morality. His economic rights have become moral rights. The legislator looking at it
sees that the blanket is made of Cellophane, he
sees through it all, but the man who brings him
this package doesn't. Neither side can give
ground without having a sense of guilt about it.
The legislator stands between. His task is to get
these people together, when either one of them,
given his way, would make it so that the other
man could have none of his way. When that happens abroad we call it dictatorship. And in every
one of us who has any idealistic drive, there is
always a little dictator who sees his own interest
as more sacred than anybody else's, who can't
cross over to the middle of the road without
blaming himself for doing so.

"The legislator is the custodian of the consciences of men so good that they ought not to
be allowed to carry their consciences with them;

they are dangerous, like loaded guns. And it's his job to bring those men together. And through wiles that he knows a little about, he talks, and talks, and talks, until they say, 'For God's sake, if you will just stop the palaver we will give in.' What has happened? By means of much talk, a little intimidation and what else not, the legislator finally gets them together. Each one goes away feeling that he did wrong and saying to himself, 'I gave up more than was right for me to give up to that so-and-so.' Nobody is happy about it; each feels that the other got the better of the bargain. Both blame the legislator who arranged this; neither of them sees, ordinarily, that while the final product was without a doubt shoddy, nine times out of ten the reason that it was shoddy was that the two sides so oversimplified and overmoralized their cases that the legislator, as a middleman who did more or less understand both of them because he had to, wasn't allowed to do the best he could in effecting a compromise. Everybody talks about the shoddiness of the output of the democratic legislative mill, which is true enough when seen from the shining cliffs of perfection. But when seen as the legislator constantly sees it, it looks like a blessed product that has all the virtues of a morality that is above what good men and good women can ever allow, because their morality is one-sided.

The legislator, as the professional compromiser, becomes thus the secular saint of our civilization, mediating between groups and saving for common ends the dynamic elements bent upon mutual destruction.

"I have seen the galleries packed with people on relief who have made up their minds that they will not peacefully stand the lowering of their already low standard of living and at the same time I have heard the taxpayers' group saying, 'We will not permit one more iota of taxation to support these loafers'—then the lines of Robert Frost have come back to my mind:

> 'Some say the world will end in fire,
>   Some say in ice.
> From what I've tasted of desire
>   I hold with those who favor fire.
> But if it had to perish twice,
>   I think I know enough of hate
> To say that for destruction ice
>   Is also great
> And would suffice.'

"The only men that habitually stand between the icy stare of those who belong to the privileged group, and the developing fiery frenzy of the other group, are the legislators in the city councils and the state legislatures and Congress. They are the only ones who ever see this situation with any degree of continuity because it involves a recognition that few people want to make, that the conflicts of life are, for the most part, as real as they seem. The results of compromising those conflicts are never very pleasing to anybody, not even to the legislator himself. According to William James, democracy is a process in which you do something and wait to see who howls; and then go and remedy the howling, waiting to see who howls from the remedy, and on and on, ever repeated so. The legislator is the humble instrument of the democratic process at the low level where the remedying deed is done."

CHAPTER VI

JUDGES, EXPERTS AND ADMINISTRATORS

IF IN a practicing democracy the legislators are the arbitrators-in-chief, makers of the treaties between regions, occupations, classes, groups, which define the current version of the general welfare, the judges, as umpires of particular disputes arising under these general definitions, play a comparably important part and a part whose effectiveness is enhanced by their strategic Constitutional position in the American system.

The rapid coming of the industrial era has especial implications for the judiciary. The wheels of industrial production were already gathering momentum when Sir Henry Maine announced that the evolution from status to contract was complete, and the legal state therefore at hand. In the hundred years that have followed, the momentum thus generated has moved society over into new and unchartered areas. The social relationships that were expressed through the legal state are being succeeded and to some extent have already been succeeded by social relationships that are struggling for expression through the welfare state.

The new situation confronts the judiciary with the problem of finding pertinent precedents. Because of the weight given to precedent in the legal process, particularly in countries like the United States where common law underlies the legislative statutes, the efficiency of the judiciary is obviously likely to be greatest in periods when the things and the processes of daily life are so familiar that the mind of man runneth not to the contrary. In modern industrial society the things of daily life change so fast that from year to year the mind of man cannot conceive of the wonders to come. Kaleidoscopic changes, both in kind and in number of the material objects that form the basis of property, are the outward sign of equal changes in the property relationships of production, distribution and exchange which the courts are called upon to sanction. Corresponding revisions are required of the concepts of property which the courts held during the period of the legal state, and which the Constitution-makers assumed prior to the courts.

One hundred and fifty years ago, when the Constitution was drawn up, discussion of the place of the judiciary in the industrial system was unthinkable. At that time, the word "industry" was understood as a quality of the ant or the bee that the sluggard might well emulate; the function of the courts was regarded as listening to law suits between private litigants and disposing of those particular suits. Today, the word industry is no longer used chiefly to define a quality; industry has grown into a very substantial system. Economic activities have been taken out of the home and organized into a vast economic empire, and they have become so enmeshed that the welfare of each depends upon the whole, and alternations of prosperity and depression affect the entire community. In the operation of this industrial system the judiciary has come to have a very distinct place. It is interesting, therefore, to inquire how the transition came about.

Statistical analysis is not a very helpful aid in understanding an institution because such analysis breaks it into parts, and then into other parts, and the end result is a diagram of a structure, and generally a structure whose function was performed long ago and now belongs to the past. But if the scholar contents himself with being a simple storyteller and saying, "Once upon a time, and then, and then, and then," he will eventually make it clear how something came into existence which never would have been planned, which was not the creation of one man or group of men but emerged out of countless generations meeting the problems with which they were face to face.

Now it is probably going too far to say that because quarrels between neighbors were settled by ordeal in England in the days when England was a sheep pasture, the United States Supreme Court behaves the way it does at the present time. But the customs of that era have indubitably done something to fix the pattern under which the United States Supreme Court exercises its over-lordship over the American industrial system. Before the word "law" came to mean what the word means today, grievances were settled for the most part by ordeal. There was a tilt, there were combatants, there was an umpire to judge, and right was on the side of the winner. Little by little trial by ordeal gave way to trial by law, but the patterns of trial by ordeal were taken over into the legal patterns, so that when the law court emerged, truth was still found and justice done in terms of combat. There were and are two parties to the combat, the plaintiff and the de-fendant, with a champion for each, the attorneys on the two sides; a judge is there with the func-tion of seeing that the rules of the combat are properly observed: he is, in other words, the umpire. And the jury has come into existence. The witnesses are for the most part clansmen, though no longer armed with staves or lances; they perform the duty of swearing for those whom they represent.

New issues come before the Court only indi-rectly. The United States Supreme Court would

refuse to consider the general legality of minimum wages, shortened hours or collective bargaining imposed upon employer and employee,
on the grounds that the big questions are not
matters of its concern. The big questions belong
to the legislature, and, within the terms marked
out by legislation, to the appropriate administrative agencies. In their general form, they cannot
be taken into court. They can be taken into court
only when a controversy occurs, and then only
when it is necessary to settle that controversy. If
a suit is filed before a court, and in such terms
that one of the big questions has to be raised,
then and only then will the courts of original
jurisdiction give attention. The United States
Supreme Court, however, is not a court of original
jurisdiction but one of appellate jurisdiction. And
appeal from a trial court to an appeal court is
never on the ground of justice, but on the ground
that mistakes were made in applying the rules of
the game down below.

To illustrate: not long ago the United States
Supreme Court, through the bench as a whole,
handed down a decision in a case involving the
conviction of a Negro in a state court for murder.
The argument was made that the Negro had not
had justice, not because the finding of the Court
was wrong but because the rules had not been
properly applied. The particular rule that had

not been properly applied concerned the fact that no Negro had sat upon the jury which declared for conviction and that no Negro had been in the panel from which the jury was chosen. No question was raised about the guilt of the person in question, no suggestion was made that if the trial were held again the same result would not be reached; the case was taken to the United States Supreme Court because of the failure of the court below to obey a technical rule. In other words, the court below was being tried for not being a fair umpire in application of the rules. The question before the Supreme Court was not primarily the question of the guilt or innocence of the person who had been convicted, it was rather the question of rules. After deliberation, the Supreme Court laid down a general rule binding upon state courts as well as Federal courts, that where Negroes constitute a substantial portion of the population, Negroes must not be excluded from jury service.

Now in theory what the Court was doing in this instance was settling a particular case; but when a particular case is made the basis of a general rule, the result is the same as legislation. So it has happened that just as language is created, just as little by little common law comes into existence, little by little the United States Supreme Court and the lower courts have woven a fabric of usages which gives them a very definite place in the economic order.

The judiciary is now performing at least four functions of major importance to the industrial system. First of these is its action to fix limits of social legislation, to place the line which says "thus far and no farther" in legislating for the public weal, to define the subjects upon which statutes can be based. That function is not assigned the Court directly in the Constitution. Before the Civil War very little was said about a definite limit upon social legislation. The limit came after the Fourteenth Amendment was added to the Constitution, the Fourteenth Amendment which forbids a state to deny to a person life, liberty, or property without due process of law. The Fourteenth Amendment was put in at the end of the Civil War as a complement to the Thirteenth, which freed the Negro, and as a precedent to the Fifteenth, which says that suffrage shall not be restricted on account of race or color. Its close relationship to the other two Amendments is indicated by the fact that all of its sections concern reconstruction matters except the first. And the last section is very significant, that Congress shall have power by appropriate legislation to enforce the provisions of this amendment.

It was understood at the time that the object

of the Amendment was to see that Southern
whites did not impose upon the Negroes who
had recently been their slaves. But the first court
case that came up under the Amendment and
most of the succeeding cases had nothing to do
with the status of the Negro. The first case came
from Louisiana at a time when the carpetbag
legislature had established monopoly of meat
packing in the City of New Orleans, excluding
all butchers who did not belong to the municipal
corporation from the practice of their particular
profession. The Southern whites had lost the war;
the Southern whites had lost at the polls; but they
saw in the Fourteenth Amendment an opportunity to turn against the enemy a section of the
Constitution which had been put there to keep
them in their place. A very able lawyer argued
before the Supreme Court that life, liberty and
property included the pursuit of happiness. One
could not pursue happiness unless he had a trade;
one could not have a trade if the trade was closed
to him; the closing of the meat-packing trade to
the butcher was therefore contrary to the Fourteenth Amendment. Moreover, it was closed in
favor of an iniquitous corporation. So a plea
for the rights of man as against a corporate monopoly was read into the Constitution.

Little by little, however, over a period of more
than twenty years, the particular formula estab-

lished by this initial case was reversed. At first
the new version commanded only four votes out
of nine. Eventually after it had been in dissent
for some years, it commanded a majority of the
votes; and by that time the rights of man had
been commuted into the privileges of corporations. Little by little, the Fourteenth Amendment
has become a charter of corporate privilege
against legislation passed by the states on behalf
of the people.

By 1905, the formula was full-fledged in its
latter form. In that year there came before the
Supreme Court an act of the State of New York,
which limited the hours of bakers to ten in any
one day. The act was challenged as unconstitu-
tional by the bakery companies. The majority of
the Court declared: first, that limitation of hours
violated the freedom of contract which was pro-
tected under the Fourteenth Amendment, and,
second, that the legislation in question was beyond the power of the legislature. In dissent, Mr.
Justice Harlan upheld the legislation, saying that
he could not persuade himself that there was any
question in economics which up to that particular
moment could be set down as eternal verity; Mr.
Justice Holmes, in one of the most conspicuous
dissenting opinions ever spread upon the record,
said that the United States Constitution does not
embody Herbert Spencer's "Social Studies" nor

any theory either of laissez-faire or of paternalism; that the legislature is therefore the proper judge of the proper boundaries of legislation, and that those boundaries would probably have to be drawn much more widely than most of his colleagues would prefer.

Since that time almost every piece of social legislation has had to run the ordeal of the courts and be weighed in terms of the abridgment of liberty or freedom of contract on the one hand and the extension of the common good on the other, and has prevailed or failed to prevail according to the value which the Court has accorded the two weights.

These weights have changed a great deal from time to time. They have varied with the personnel of the Court. They have varied with good times and bad times. And as the country has gone farther and farther away from laissez-faire, and come to appreciate more and more the need for administration, the shift has very definitely been more and more in favor of finding statutes valid. At the moment the tendency is for the judiciary not to interpose nearly as much as heretofore in setting limits beyond which social legislation shall not go, but the possibility of its exercising that function nevertheless remains.

A second function of the Federal judiciary in the industrial system is to serve as umpire of the

Federal system, drawing the line between Federal authority and state authority. With recognition that the current operation of the market produces economic results less satisfactory than those anticipated by exponents of laissez-faire, economic phenomena such as sweatshops, monopolies or gentlemen's agreements about prices, long hours, discriminatory railroad rates, export fluctuations affecting domestic supply, and the like have become recognized liabilities in the industrial process, and legislative efforts have been made to eliminate them.

Most of the early statutes passed were state statutes. When the businesses affected by them went to court in an effort to prove their own acts lawful, and the acts of the legislature unlawful, they appealed to the Federal courts on the ground that the matter in question concerned interstate commerce and was therefore beyond the power of the legislature of a particular state. The records show this line of argument arising in the last part of the seventies, continuing through the eighties, increasing in the nineties, and prevalent everywhere around 1900.

After that date, however, it became increasingly clear that state legislation was impotent to deal with conditions in coal and oil and railroads and the like, and national legislation began to be used. The tenor of the contesting briefs was then reversed; all efforts on the part of the contending companies were bent on showing that the business in question was intra-state and therefore beyond the reach of Federal legislation.

The proponents of laissez-faire have thus bulwarked their efforts to hold government intervention to a minimum, first by expressing a concern for national unity and then by championing state rights. For this important series of disputes, the Supreme Court has been umpire.

A third function of the United States Supreme Court is to fix the limits of collective activity. When the great web of American Constitutional law was, little by little, being woven, the country was new and there was a frontier. Individual enterprise and laissez-faire were more or less the order of the day, and affected the rulings of the Court along with other social activities. Then the question came up as to how far groups can extend their activities and still stay within the law; how far a group of businessmen can go in an industry, how far a group of laborers can go in a union, how far a group of farmers can go in a co-operative. The function of fixing the limits of legal tolerance of collective activity fell eventually to the judiciary. For a long time the pattern of action sanctioned by the judiciary was an individual one. It was most individualistic in connection with labor unions: it virtually denied to collective

bargaining any protection of the law. The individualistic pattern was less rigidly imposed in
respect to farmers' co-operatives, which were allowed a great deal more tolerance than labor organizations. The story of the action of the judiciary in connection with groups of businessmen
is a complicated one. In cases of alleged price-
fixing or restraint of trade, the burden of proof
is on the government; the cases have been pro-
tracted in the extreme, with one procedural issue
after another raised in order to defer consideration of the real elements in the case. The Sherman Act was passed in 1890; in 1938 the total
amount of fines collected under it is still less
than two million dollars.

Moreover, the choice of procedures open to the
government in prosecuting such cases has been
such as to obscure the issue. Under the Sherman
Act, two forms of enforcement are possible. Individuals can be indicted under the criminal law
for violating the Act, or petition can be made to
the courts for an injunction to restrain their practices. It is far more efficient to indict under the
criminal law, because rather than be tagged as
criminals people will make a great many con-
cessions, whereas a simple suit in equity, without
any threat of criminal proceedings, can be turned
off on procedural questions and allowed to drag
on year after year. Yet the real question with

which the government and the judiciary are faced
is not a question of moral conduct, of whether
or not certain individuals should go to jail; it
is a question of the social effect of the pattern of
a basic industry, and how tolerant the government is going to be of that pattern.

The problems of the judiciary in deciding these
questions are enormously complicated by the variety of existing industrial patterns. One of the
reasons given for the decision in the N.R.A. case
was that Congress had not been sufficiently definite in setting up standards to which industry
should adhere, as if there were a norm that cov-
ered all industry, as if friction were located at the
same point in all industries. But only a brief
glance at the structures of only one group of industries, those connected with motor transport,
shows how the incidence of industrial maladjust-
ment may vary.

The pattern of the automobile industry was
established about 1910. Refusal of investment
bankers to lend money prevented the automobile
concerns from manufacturing all the parts that
make up a car. For that reason they farmed their
parts out. Because they had no money to set up
retail outlets, they engaged independent dealers.
With the retailing and parts-manufacturing out
of the picture their own operations were limited
to the assembly line. Little by little work on the

line was made more mechanical. Because it was made mechanical, practically no skilled labor was used, and for some time labor problems did not exist. That was the early pattern of the industry. When trouble came it was along two fronts. Friction developed with the dealers. Friction likewise developed with the workers. The unskilled workers in the plants had been able to do nothing so long as they were unorganized. Even after they became organized, if they walked out the company could walk others in and train them so fast that six weeks later everything would be running as smoothly as before, because the tasks were unskilled. Then the workers invented the sit-down strike and found a weapon they had not had before.

In the tire industry, the larger concerns began by marketing their own products. Then the mail-order houses went into the game with their methods of distribution and set prices that the manufacturing companies could not equal. Friction in the tire industry is at the point of competition between dealer-controlled outlets and the mail-order houses.

In gasoline, an overbuilt retail structure has set up retail outlets glaring at each other from every corner. A comparable structure exists in the oil fields, with offset wells around property lines. Somewhere in between there is something of a

chance for monopoly. The problem of the petro-
leum industry is not whether there is competition
or monopoly, but where competition lies and
where monopoly lies.

These instances make it clear that industrial
regulation, to be effective, must get down to concrete cases; that the time of patent medicine is
very definitely past; and that the courts must look
at industry in terms of the web of trade usage that
has grown up in each particular industry and try
to direct that usage to social ends rather than to
impose a blueprint called the law of competition
on the affairs of various industries.

In fulfilling the three functions so far mentioned, the judiciary has had the task of limiting
the field of social action, determining what Mr.
Keynes has called the agenda or nonagenda of
government. Following periods of enlargements
of those boundaries, the focus of interest is likely
to shift to the public bodies in charge of the administration of statutes whose validity has been
upheld. There seems some probability that in the
immediate future the fourth function of the Supreme Court, judicial supervision of the work of
administrative bodies, will be its most prominent
activity.

The growth of the administrative arm of government is probably the most spectacular change
which the industrial era has made in the political

field. It is clear that without expert assistance neither the legislative nor the judicial arm of government can maintain the concurrent contact required for wise policy-making in respect to myriad industrial patterns of organization. One of the Interstate Commerce Commissioners made the comment in a rate case that this was a play at which the Supreme Court takes an occasional look from the balcony, but the Commissioners have seats in the orchestra for every performance.

Under such circumstances, the need of the courts for technical advice is clear. So far the need has been better met with respect to the legislature than with respect to the judiciary. The device of House and Senate committee-hearings to make available to Congress the technical resources of the Departments of the Federal Government and the findings of private agencies has not been paralleled by the provision of similar facilities for the courts. Yet the need for judicial understanding of administrative procedure is rapidly growing. The courts have come a long way from trial by ordeal and from individualistic justice, but their tradition is still to look upon cases as private affairs between private parties, and to ignore the extent to which the private parties may be symbols of much larger forces and thereby make the judges umpires of a much larger game.

English experience shows the importance of recognition by the judiciary of certain essential differences between judicial and administrative procedure. The years just prior to the World War saw the passage, in rapid succession, of a series of social security laws under which administrative personnel and administrative functions were greatly augmented. The view was expressed in some quarters that the increasing exercise of power by administrative agencies put citizens' liberties in danger of having to be rewon. In 1911 a case—Local Government Board v. Arlidge, dealing with the demolition of a house as unfit for human habitation—showed the inappropriateness of both the judicial and the administrative procedure then current, and the desirability of establishing a procedure that partook of both functions. Statutes since that time have generally recognized the following principles:

1. The citizen shall have a clear statement of what the government proposes to do.

2. He shall have opportunity to present evidence on his own behalf and to hear the evidence presented on behalf of the State.

3. He shall have access to the report made by the administrative agent of the government and an opportunity to present his point of view on the report.

4. After compliance with these provisions, the action to be taken becomes a matter of administrative discretion.

The establishment in the United States of a comparable understanding of the difference in the nature of the two processes, judicial and administrative, is of the first importance to efficient government. In the long run, the influence of the spectacular decisions of the Supreme Court on the daily course of the administrative process is probably less than that of the cumbersome procedure, technical rules, delays and confusion of interest in the intent of parties with interest in the effect of their action on the body politic which occur when administrative procedure is forced into the judicial mold.

If there is even a grain of truth in the aphorism, "Government is only one-tenth popular—the rest is administrative," it is essential for the administrative branch of the government to develop its own type, its own genius, its own formula for efficiency suitable to the new types of economic behavior with which it has to deal.

Part of the formula for good administration clearly consists in the working out of a proper relationship with the judiciary; no less fundamental is the working out of a comparable relationship with the legislative and the executive—a problem to which the division of powers in the American system adds peculiar difficulties. Both the politician and the administrator need to recognize that there is as definite a difference between the function of the public policy maker and that of the civil servant as there is between the function of the civil servant and that of the judge.

Legislators and chief executives come and go. It is the function of the administrative branch to provide the necessary element of governmental continuity by serving as the storehouse of governmental experience from which each incoming administration can draw.

Part of the essential skill of the politician is to know the needs and desires of the constituents in the political jurisdiction which he serves. The objectives of public policy are his specialty. But in the complexities of the modern world the means of attaining each specific objective is a subject with which only a technical specialist can cope. The civil servant's field is this field of specialized knowledge; his job is to supply the policy makers with the facts and experience which are his by virtue of day-to-day contact with the parts of the national life which are on the legislative agenda for the immediate future, or which have been past subjects of legislative action.

It is then the function of the legislator, or of the executive when preparing legislation to propose to Congress, to relate the information ob-

tained from the administrative staff to the demands of his constituents for the achievement of
certain social objectives. It is his function to see
that there is broad popular discussion of the specialist's findings, so that the facts found in the
laboratory may also be found in the street, so that
changes in social organization proposed by social
engineers can be interrelated and integrated with
the general on-going organization of society.

Joint performance of these functions by legislator and specialist is prerequisite to democratic
action. When an issue first makes itself felt, there
are likely to be several groups of competing
"facts" in the field, each advanced as the truth by
one of the parties to the dispute and accompanied
by a proposed solution. Only after analysis of the
various alleged facts by the civil servant, and
brokerage among the competing interests by the
legislator in the light of that analysis, can action
be taken in terms agreed upon by all parties.

Close relationship between the various departments of the Federal Government and Congress,
and effective functioning of the staffs attached to
the legislative advisory councils which are being
developed in an increasing number of states, is
particularly important in view of the extent to
which lobbying has been developed in the past.
Most of the country's big corporations employ
staffs of specialists to keep up with current scien-

tific findings pertinent to the company's interests, and legislative representatives to impress those findings on Congressmen and members of state legislatures. The high pressure which they apply creates a danger of underrepresentation of other interests in the country which are no less real for being less highly organized; it becomes the function of the civil service to provide the legislators with the necessary materials for maintaining a balanced view.

The division of powers specified in the Federal Constitution makes the construction of a bridge between Congress and the technical services of the Departments and other administrative agencies a matter whose delicacy is comparable to its importance. In the view of some men of experience, it is possible for adequate communication between Congress and the Secretaries and staffs of the Departments to be maintained through the Congressional Committees. In view of others, the fact that the administrative services are agents of the executive renders them unavoidably suspect in the eyes of the legislators and blocks the flow which would otherwise be possible from existing reservoirs of technical advice. Holders of this view would prefer to see Cabinet Members drawn from Congress, or at any rate subject to question and debate on the floor of Congress, so that a unity now lacking could be fostered as a prelude to national legislation.

Whatever the means by which closer relationships between the technical and the policy-making branches of government are established, the necessity for recognition of its essentially advisory role remains the same. The agenda of government are not its affair; its task is to give the policy makers advice distilled from specific technical findings on the results of the government's various programs currently in operation, on the probable effects of proposed changes in the programs, on how desired changes can best be brought about. It is the duty of the civil service to present its findings to the policy makers, and reiterate them with vigor in case they prove distasteful and are disregarded. Further than that, however, administrative officials should not go: direct contact by technicians with outsiders regarding an administration which in their view is going off at a tangent disregards lines of responsibility with results which in the long run prove bad. A British technician in the Ministry of Health was once asked: "Suppose the Government asked for advice on how to create slums instead of how to eliminate them, what would be your function?" He replied, "It would be to create slums or resign."

For to the extent that the Civil Service sets up its own will in contradistinction to the will of the elected policy makers, power is detracted from the representative system and the beginnings of a bureaucracy are at hand. The experience of the Weimar Republic exemplified the clash between a popularly elected government and a Civil Service which believed itself to be custodian of the Staatsinn—the sense of the State as a whole—and as such to stand above and beyond the give-and-take of the daily struggle for power. To a Civil Service in that mood, the safeguarding of its position becomes a major objective, and its activities partake more and more of the nature of irresponsible government. Unless the administrative branch of the government remains loyal to the political institutions of the country, charges of bureaucracy will not only be made, but will be true.

CHAPTER VII

CONTEMPORARY DEMOCRACY AND CONTEMPORARY AGRICULTURE

THE preceding pages have suggested some of the changes, the problems, the proposals of which contemporary agriculture must take account. The new world in which agriculture must find its place is a fully settled country. The completion of continental settlement has solidified the social structure so that the outlines of its various aspects can be recognized, and new interests and new emphases are the result.

The spatially expanding universe in which Americans of the nineteenth century lived weakened their sense of any sort of form. Existing national objectives, like existing national resources, were suffused by the glow of an anticipated El Dorado somewhere beyond the horizon. Things without limit were things without outline. And at the same time that the larger concepts of national life were exhibiting the formlessness of the unexplored continent, the familiar objects of everyday use took on the repetitious patterns of factory mass production. Consequently, after the sun of acquisition had followed the frontier down

into the cold Pacific, and the afterglow of the new
economic era had given way to the darkness of
the depression, there was considerable groping for
the shape of things to come.

The nineteenth-century manner of living also
restricted the average American's sense of time—
he lived for the here and now. Time was the present and the immediate future tense; time was a
state of economic becoming fully expressed by
the slogan "Get Rich Quick." America was the
melting pot whose unity was to be found in the
present and future, not in the diverse origins of
the past. Everything was so new that the richness
of tradition was not seen as a contributor to current wealth. But this contemporaneity of American life could not last. With the passage of time,
the New World has become older, and the value
placed upon experience has grown. The American
government of today is one of the oldest forms of
government in the world in the sense of unbroken
service. And in recent years the sense of being a
people that have weathered past trials together is
increasingly relied on as a source of strength for
trials to come.

The growing recognition of an American tradition extending through time, and an American
style of organization covering the things of the
world of space, has placed fresh importance both
on the long-term values which have given, and

give, cohesion and unity to American life, and on
current techniques for organizing the social structure.

The patterns of action and the structure and
mechanism of operation, of both private groups
and public bodies, have recently taken on a significance unknown in the United States since the
Constitution-making period. The New World is
increasingly aware of organization by economic
groups, groups of businessmen, of factory workers, of farmers. The new consciousness of the existence of the state is being reflected in new political organization as various groups, farmers,
workers and others, seek to accumulate and use
political power to redress the balance of economic
power. Today, expectations of increases in the
nation's economic wealth are based, not on further appropriation of unclaimed resources, but
upon better organization of resources already
claimed.

In the realm of the values necessary to national
unity, the last few years have warned of the dangers of the nineteenth-century concentration on
the values of the acquisitive life to the practical
exclusion of other values. The full dinner pail as
a national objective has been recognized as a
vitally necessary but far too partial emphasis upon
bread alone; for the converse of that slogan is

that a nation that does not have prosperity has nothing.

Without prosperity, a nation that has no other commonly held aim will cease to be a nation. The have-nots will organize around the nineteenth-century objective that equates the good life with a rising standard of living. The haves will organize around a pseudo-religious ideal similar to the myth of the Nazis, using the glory of the national being as a façade to economic coercion. A house so divided against itself cannot stand.

A nation, to be a nation, must have a common fund of mutual confidence and a common experience of agreed procedure on which to draw in times of economic and other exigency. In the United States, from the beginning of American history, the common fund has been the democratic faith, and the agreed procedure has been the democratic process.

But there has been too little common experience of the agreed procedure, and American democracy has too often exhibited the weakness of faith without works. If Thomas Jefferson could have walked the rural highways and byways and visited with the farmers of the United States in the past fifty or seventy-five years, it is possible that he would have shaken his head when he recalled saying that American government will remain virtuous as long as the country is chiefly ag-

ricultural. The general philosophy of democracy
has been there, but the practice of democracy has
been too largely absent. Too little thought has
been given, and consequently too little action has
been taken, to find ways whereby the average
farmer would participate in the democratic processes of an increasingly complex society. The prestige and the socially desirable prizes of life in a
farm community have been largely confined to
success in operating an individual farm enterprise. The folkways of nineteenth-century America, indeed of America up through the World
War, directed men's endeavor more and more exclusively into the field of economic action. As
economic emphasis shifted from farming to factory production, industrial success, personified in
the "captains of industry," became the object of
general respect. At the same time the affairs of
government declined in prestige and the politician became the object of frequent caricature.
City success was such a magnet that every year it
drew hundreds of thousands of boys and girls
away from the farms; those who stayed on in the
country tried to do on the farm the thing that
was most like what was being done in the city.
And they were generally content to leave politics
and the affairs of government to the lawyers, to
the professional politicians; to assume that the

farmer's business was primarily to be a successful farmer.

For this reason, American farmers, as they evolved from the simple agricultural frontier, did not seem to have a deep, abiding concern for participation in democratic processes. Rural government, county government and state government went on, but the number of farmers who had aggressive, individual concern about their local government, about the other levels of government, and about the policies under which they lived their lives, were not very many; there were not very many farmer members of Congress. Very few of the agricultural educators of the last generation were thinking in terms of the total democratic pattern or of a rural civilization. The education offered in the agricultural colleges was focused primarily on biological science, on the techniques of agricultural production, and on the vocational side of agriculture. But given the current concern with broader matters, it seems probable that agricultural democracy is in the process of working out more practical demonstrations of its philosophy than have been prevalent in the recent past.

First among needs in such a development is an inventory of the functioning of agricultural democracy in the United States, an analysis of the current workings of the democratic process in communities and in states and with reference to national agricultural programs and the share of agriculture in American society.

Such an inventory should concern itself with a variety of questions: What are the patterns of ideas, both in the realm of tradition and folklore and in the realm of rational thought, under which farm communities live at the present time? What are possible types of patterns for the democratic way of life that might be appropriate twenty-five or fifty years from now?

To what extent, quantitatively speaking, do farmers participate in the affairs of community, county, state and national government? Where there is participation, is it chiefly by the upper third of the farmers?

What percentage of farmers have thought in an intelligent truth-searching way about problems of national welfare and agricultural policy? How much are farmers being influenced by the propaganda of national pressure groups? Do farmers who have had the advantages of agricultural education in vocational high schools, colleges of agriculture, or agricultural extension work, differ greatly in their functioning as citizens from farmers who have not had these advantages?

To what extent are farmers in a frame of mind to participate in agricultural planning in their counties and communities, to develop programs for improving agriculture through use of available scientific data and the collaboration of experts?

How democratic is the procedure of the national farm organizations? To what extent are the national agricultural programs now in effect the outgrowth of local policy-making by farm groups? Has their operation stimulated and developed democratic patterns of behavior?

To what extent is there mutual understanding of each other's problems on the part of rural and urban people? What institutions are acting to broaden this understanding?

The answers to these questions concern all sorts of American citizens. They concern the individual farmer in the local farm community. They concern the staffs of the great national farm organizations. They concern the public officials related to agriculture, whether as educators, technicians, administrators or politically responsible men.

The local community is the place where the democracy of the nation will stand its ultimate test. In a country the size of the United States, representative institutions are an obvious necessity, and the problems requiring governmental action over broad areas are many. But representative institutions are only a device for carrying forward the policies which individual citizens arrive at through direct participation in areas small

enough to make direct participation possible.
Representative institutions can operate only when
the representatives have something to represent,
something worked out on the ground that forms
their constituency, and something that covers all
of that ground. In communities where democracy
functions, the difficult process of hearing all sides,
weighing the main arguments, maintaining minds
open to persuasion, and participating in the give-
and-take of final agreement leads on to government by the people. Representatives from such
communities go up to their legislatures with a
mandate to which adequate local thought has
been given.

The alternative to government by the people is
government for the people. The mandate given
to its representatives by a local community may
be based upon collective consideration of current
policies. But another basis of representation is
wholly possible. Citizens whom local institutions
leave out of consideration accumulate grievances
which are intensified because no provision is made
for them to be expressed. Such citizens have no
local habitation; they long for change without
access to the means by which changes are made.
Then along will come a leader who puts into
words the pent-up emotion which their grievances
have gathered. He will get things done for them;
and they in turn will give him their allegiance,

give him a mystical mandate which has little in common with the mandate received by a representative in a functioning democracy. Through him, the inarticulate fractions of the community will hope to find strength to coerce into change the local institutions which have given them no place.

In communities where substantial numbers of citizens look elsewhere for salvation, self-government ceases and democracy fails. Obviously, many problems which are locally acute are problems which must be attacked by agencies larger than the local community as well as by the local community. Only through coherent, co-operative effort at various governmental levels can adequate solutions to such problems be obtained. But the health of the whole of a democracy is maintained through the health of its parts.

The postwar experience of the agricultural areas of the country may be cited in this connection. The shift in the international position of the United States from debtor to creditor, and the sudden disappearance of the foreign markets for American foodstuffs which had existed ever since the continent was opened up and which had been greatly augmented by the War, were events far removed from the daily life on American farms. Yet they affected directly the future of those farms. In such an exigency, governmental measures to relieve the situation were certain to be taken. But the measures could be framed and executed so as to be either government for, or government by, the people. The years since the War have made it abundantly clear that as changing national and world conditions require national policies by the Federal Government in agriculture, and as Congress develops new national programs, the national aspects of these programs must be offset by proportionately increased individual participation by the farmer and his family in the formation of the national policy and in its local administration. It is a condition of sound democracy that each individual farmer develop a new individual responsibility for himself and for his community which parallels the new responsibility placed upon the Federal Government.

The county planning committees which have developed in increasing numbers in the past few years bear witness to the extent to which farmers are assuming these new responsibilities. A number of counties have long traditions of planning for county affairs: in certain localities, the habit of local consideration of the public welfare runs all the way back to colonial town meetings or county courts; in others, general planning has developed out of the agricultural crisis of the years since the War. Such county groups have demonstrated and are demonstrating the possibility of democratic social control as a vital alternative to authoritarian rule from above.

The rapid development of county boards of strategy is particularly striking in view of the emergency action which had to be taken in 1933. The programs then inaugurated to meet the crisis, which was fast turning into catastrophe, were for the most part highly centralized. They expressed a farm opinion on the type of action needed which had been developing for some years, but their first phases represented quick action by Congress and the Department of Agriculture. The different programs inaugurated to meet the emergency at different points consequently reached the field in forms which were not integrated so far as the local communities were concerned. The establishment of local committees by such agencies as the Agricultural Adjustment Administration and the Resettlement Administration was a first step immediately taken for the relation of general policy to local conditions. A further step, more recently taken, to combine the county activities under these two action programs with general discussion of agricultural welfare, has been described by one of the agricultural leaders concerned as follows:

"It appeared that local initiative and leadership could be restored and the groundwork laid for a mass agricultural movement which would take

advantage of all the assistance now available to
agriculture in establishing a new standard of social and economic well-being through a truly
democratic process. But we realized that these
three major activities necessarily would be combined into one well-co-ordinated program and
that something more than the preparation of land-
use maps, the formulation of statistical tables on
adjusted production, and the holding of interesting but rather pointless discussions would have
to be done. After due consideration of the difficulties involved, the unlimited amount of work
required, and the possible advantages of such a
procedure, we finally made the rather bold decision of uniting these three programs into one
procedure and adding three or four other features: first, organization of permanent county
boards of agriculture with committees in each
community representing all geographic areas, all
types of farming and the programs of all agencies;
second, establishment of a professional council in
each county to include the public employees of
all agricultural agencies, and to serve in an advisory capacity to the county boards of agriculture; third, to maintain a far-reaching program of
adult education throughout each county by making the community committees of each county
board responsible for the organization and conduct of discussion groups in each community; and

finally, when land resources have been mapped, community discussions conducted, and conferences held between agency representatives and planning committees, to extend the plans prepared and the policies established into practical application through action programs planned and directed in every community by the community committeemen."

Local activities such as these provide direct contact between the technicians and administrators engaged in work on agricultural programs and the actual people for whose welfare the programs were established. The general laws which set up agricultural programs express what the representatives of the general public believe to be the general welfare. The specific administration of the law is a specific concern of the administrators and the particular groups for whom the laws were intended as a direct benefit. If the administrators are not in close touch with the people whom their actions affect, a bureaucracy may develop and the only recourse of the people under it may be to appeal to the general public to revoke the general law. Still more important in terms of day-to-day activity is the fact that under most general laws various alternatives in respect to specific administrative practices are equally legal. The democratic process can operate in the making of choices between such alternatives. The technicians and

administrators will have something to say on the
subject, and should be allowed to say it. But the
people concerned will also have something to say
on the subject, and it is vital that they be heard.
The county planning committees are providing
this hearing.

Examples of the type of decisions in which local
people are playing an indispensable part along
with the technicians and administrators cover a
wide range. For instance, in connection with the
programs aimed at eliminating some of the evils
of tenancy, certain local criteria have to be established. What constitutes an economic family unit
under the particular farm conditions of this locality? Should controlled bank accounts be established in which tenant purchasers are required to
deposit a share of their cash crop proceeds in
order to assure their having funds for taxes, insurance and loan repayments as these fall due? In
what counties of the state should loans be made?
What is an equitable division of loans as between
Negro and white farmers? At what value should
farms be appraised? What families should be recommended for loans? How large should the loans
be? Farm people who serve on boards which seek
and find answers to questions such as these are
practicing democrats. A nation built of local communities where such activities are going on is a

nation where the roots of democracy are thrust deep into fertile soil.

Active participation by its members is essential to the health of the local community; it is no less vital to the health of private groups in which farmers participate on the basis of their occupation. Occupational organizations of farmers, factory workers, industrialists and professional men may serve democracy well if they present to the American public the attitudes, desires and policies of their members. But if they are to serve democracy, the leaders of these organizations, as the economic representatives of the men and women who belong to them, need the same type of considered mandate as the political representatives of areas where democracy is at work. Private as well as public organizations suffer from the temptation to short-circuit the democratic process through the mechanisms of caucus and manipulation. The increasing practice of farm democracy in farm organizations would seem to include an increasing effort to build the annual programs out of discussions among the members in hundreds of local groups, whose findings are passed on to larger units, and so on up to the national councils. National conventions arising out of such a process would consist of delegates with little tendency to rubber-stamp the proposals of the resolutions committee; they would magnify the type of leadership which hearty self-government develops at the expense of the type of leadership which claims to be representative because it believes that it knows what the farmers, or the business-men, or the doctors, or the trade unionists need, and proposes to give it to them.

The choice as to which type of leadership shall be offered is just as clear-cut in the case of government bodies administering farm programs as it is in the case of private organizations representing farm interests. Benevolent paternalism is perhaps even more likely to be a feature of government than of organizations whose influence is less pervasive than that of government. The tests of democratic procedure should therefore be all the more rigorously applied; answers should be continually sought to questions such as these:

To what extent have such measures as the Agricultural Adjustment Act, the Soil Conservation Act, the Farm Security Act, produced by the voting process, increased the practice of democracy in farm areas?

In the formulation of national agricultural programs, what use is made of information locally collected and judgments locally worked out?

Is the administration of the program kept close to the individual farm; is it flexible in adopting techniques appropriate to the innumerable variations from community to community?

Are local committeemen generally chosen by the farmers of their neighborhood or are they designated by local government officials?

At meetings, hearings and other assemblies of farmers are the opinions expressed on the farm programs free from official dominance?

Have the national agricultural referenda provided a genuine index of the desires of the persons involved in the pending decisions?

To what extent are the various agricultural programs administered in such a way as to educate their participants in long-run objectives as well as immediate benefits?

In order for the answers to these questions to be consistent with democratic procedure, constant attention needs to be given to the working out of a number of relationships.

One of these is the relationship between the national agencies and the localities in regard to the formulation of agricultural programs. In a country the size of the United States, the value of the regional or area approach to national problems is even greater than in most other countries. The organic character of the life of the various sections is becoming an assumption of government, with corresponding attention paid to suiting organization to the organism rather than forcing local life into artificial forms. The period of looking on regional differences as quaint sources of local color is passing; the national life is increasingly conceived as built out of a genuine diversity of customs and attitudes just as the will of a democracy is composed from a multitude of individual wills.

Under such circumstances, maintenance of the proper balance between centralization and decentralization becomes a primary consideration of government. The essential values of regional and local autonomy have to be weighed against the need for collaboration among the regions in the interest of the general welfare. Autonomy carried too far can lead to secession, just as centralization carried too far can lead to stultification of local initiative.

In concrete terms of the daily activities of agencies making agricultural programs, how should regional and local wants, and information regionally and locally compiled, be combined with nationally made estimates of facts and the requirements of the general welfare? Certain general principles have emerged from recent experience. It is of the nature of this type of program formation that at some point the information supplied and the desires expressed by the various regions have to be reconciled, and that the central administrative agency alone can do this. It is also of the nature of this type of program formation that the administrative officer should write the necessary orders only after holding hearings at which those who are to operate under the program have an opportunity to be heard. Those who operate under the program have a right to offer suggestions to the administrator, to have their suggestions duly considered by the administrator when decisions are made, and to be told why in case their recommendations are not adopted.

Where this two-way process of suggestion and revision operates, several major administrative problems are likely to be solved. The administrator at the center has little likelihood of being insulated in a remote bureau from the effects of the program in the field. Participants in the program find incentives to responsible action in the knowledge that a large part of their proposals will be put into actual practice.

The finding of the proper governmental area for the technical job to be done, be it water control, banking, social security, or agricultural adjustment, and the installation in that regional office of personnel fitted for two-way transmission between the national agency and the field, is perhaps the major task of the administrative agencies today. Ready contact between civil servant and citizen is essential—Harun al Rashid was a wise emperor when he disguised himself as a private person and walked in the city to find out what the people were thinking. The common man and woman who are affected by the administrative side of government programs should not be expected to come to Washington or write to Washington or proceed through the courts; there should be administrative offices located near enough for them to take up their problems with responsible officials face to face.

Continual give-and-take between citizens and administrators, moreover, provides the most efficient means of obtaining concurrent criticism of the work of administrative agencies, and acting on it in time. As the function of the legislature becomes increasingly a function of laying out broad general objectives, and charging the administrative agencies with the selection of means for reaching these objectives, the need for an intelligent opposition, which democratic legislatures have long recognized, becomes a need of the administrative arm. If administrative abuses are not concurrently corrected, the people suffering under them will turn for redress to their political representatives, and the legislature may abandon a sound objective because a faulty means of effecting it has been maintained in force. If abuses are concurrently corrected and alternative procedures constantly considered, there is little danger of the development of a bureaucracy which the people cannot reach.

Contact between civil service and civilians tests

the capacity of administrators not only to fulfill but also to stay within bounds of the function which they have been assigned to perform. Too much idealism can be an administrative fault. Education of the public to want something better than it is likely to demand from its current combination of ignorance, prejudice, horse sense and desire for fair play is a valid function of the civil servant, but he should not force his idealism on the public without the public's having a choice. The civil servant must proceed on mandates given through the political institutions designed for the purpose, rather than on departmental concepts of the public's good.

A further possibility of divergence between a given program as desired by the people in the localities where it is to operate, and as desired by the administrative officials charged with its operation, arises from the essential difference between plans made on the basis of scientific findings and ideas developed in the give-and-take of local political discussion. The technician thinks of policy as a precise program made to fit a precise situation, a social plan which must be adopted as a whole and unchanged during the entire period of its proposed operation. The everyday citizen, like his political representative, thinks of policy as a compromise to which people's loyalty is only contingent, as the best currently available equilibrium among various groups and interests, subject to change without notice. The potential conflict between planning and democracy indicated by this difference is a serious matter. The modern world is faced with the paradox that while science flourishes best under a democracy, science produces a complex economic system which cannot be governed by a hit-or-miss policy subject to frequent reversals.

In mitigating the consequences of this paradox the role of the upper administrative officer is most important. He is the go-between between the legislator fresh from the hustings and the scientist fresh from the laboratory or the calculating machine. The specialties of the various technicians are like a spectrum which it is his function to assemble into white light for transmittal to the policy makers, executive and legislative, with whom he is in contact. The draft bills of the policy makers are proposals whose potential usefulness it is his function to analyze in terms of the technical data available from the scientists on his staff. Somewhere in the course of these functions considerable reconciliation of scientific plans and democratic decisions can take place.

The staffing of the upper administrative post is one of the crucial tests of the operation of administrative agencies. Procedure is important to the civil service setup: intra- and inter-departmental co-ordination; general pacemaking to speed the routine of a sheltered occupation; proper routing of work and the like to provide an efficient machinery. Machinery, however, does not run by itself. Without able people at the controls it will idle or break down.

The problem of advancement from technical to administrative, and from administrative to politically responsible, positions in government agencies is one of considerable delicacy. The function of the technician is to be scientifically proficient in his specialty. The function of the administrator is to transmit technically tested light to the political officer. The function of the political officer is to use that light in the heat of the political arena. It is current American practice to rob the laboratory by turning the better scientists into administrators without great regard for qualifications which concern both training and temperament; because of the marked difference between the two functions, transfers from one to another are likely to place square pegs in round holes. Yet the fact remains that the assumption of administrative duties is the chief method of achieving economic freedom now open to the scientist, and the ladder of specialist, administrator, political officer is the hierarchy of prestige.

Particularly because the United States is a country whose tradition has only recently come to in-

clude preparation for public service, the possibilities of in-service training of administrative staffs
appear great. The test of whether various units
are maintaining a proper output, automatically
supplied at least to the smaller private businesses
by their balance sheets, is difficult to obtain in
public service. Yet in the absence of some internal
means of keeping people up to the mark, the chief
occupational disease of the civil servant, cynicism,
is apt to spread. Introductory training courses,
courses to familiarize newcomers with their work,
more advanced courses to refresh people who have
been three to five years in service, and general
discussions by the staff of the function and strategy of the agency as a whole can both stimulate
the keenness of the entire organization and guide
personnel officers in selections for administrative
advancement.

The in-service training courses of the government agencies, however, can obviously perform
only a small part of the general educational task
necessary to the proper functioning of democratic
government. The administrators of laws passed as
contributions to the general welfare clearly must
have an appreciation of the general welfare over
and above a proficiency in their particular specialty, but they are only a small part of the people,
and it is the people's capacity to recognize and
act in terms of the general welfare which in the

long run determines whether that general welfare
will be served.

The technical training through which American education has turned out specialists is clearly
not enough. Such men may do exactly what society asks of them and yet do harm to society. An
example of such harm may be seen along some
of the highways that run across the farm lands of
the country. Modern society asked the engineers
who build and maintain the highways to substitute a very arbitrary system for the old animal
trails that used to wind around in consideration
of local topography, and to grade those highways
so as to drain water off of them as fast as possible.
The engineers performed their allotted task. But
what of the consequences? One area, for example,
has an average of ten gullies to the mile running
back into farm land and cutting the farms into
sections. Now in such cases the engineers executed their work conscientiously and in good
faith, and the farmers along the highway were
probably among the first to want the roads. Yet
the engineers and the farmers co-operated in pil-
ing up a social deficit whose extent was lost upon
both until the damage was done. Today, however,
many states have acted or are now acting to co-
ordinate the social need for good roads with the
social need for good farm land. Landscape archi-
tects are now on the staffs of many state highway

departments, with the function of devising means of minimizing erosion as the nation's highways are drained. The integration of the thinking of these specialists who work in terms of minimizing the damage of run-off, with the thinking of the engineers who work in terms of getting the water to run, represents a successful solution to the type of problem which modern society faces all along the line.

The colleges of the country are showing clear signs of recognizing that the function of American education is not only to aid the student to attain proficiency in a special occupation but to help him attain a genuine understanding of the interrelations of all the special proficiencies, to give him an appreciation of the general welfare and a sense of participation in the moral and cultural values of the America of today.

The colleges of agriculture show the beginnings of a movement to reshape the education of rural youth in such a fashion as to put new emphasis on these general patterns of American civilization as opposed to mere commercial and technical efficiency. Courses in agricultural philosophy, in the social sciences and the humanities as related to farm life and farm problems, are becoming more and more basic in the preparation of students for rural life.

And the activities in rural areas of those who

have gone beyond the years of specialized agricultural training, the revival of local discussions by farm people across the length and breadth of the country, are an indication that adult education is taking on the proportions of a great popular movement, paralleling the increased public activities of farm people with an increased grasp of the general concepts in terms of which they are dealing.

The subjects chosen for these discussions, moreover, show a widening recognition of the need for cross-fertilization among the various groups in the nation's life. The group consciousness which is a more or less recent feature of American society is at the same time a consciousness that no one group can accomplish much alone. Interdependence cannot long continue in the absence of understanding. The farm group growingly realizes that an understanding of its needs, its motives and its objectives on the part of the city people who are at one and the same time consumers of its products, producers of its purchases, and fellow democrats in the American Republic is necessary alike to the achievement and to the maintenance of national measures for agricultural welfare. And the necessary converse of city understanding of farm problems is farm understanding of city problems.

The current requirements of the democratic

process in respect to farm communities, farm organizations and government agencies related to
agriculture have been graphically stated by John
R. Commons. It is his view that individualism
when carried to its logical conclusion results in
anarchy; groupism when carried to its logical
conclusion comes to be syndicalism, whereby
society degenerates into a mass of struggling
groups, each trying to annihilate the other; and
statism when carried to its logical conclusion results in state socialism. Now, democracy is each of
these three forces pressing against the other two.
It is as though individualism, groupism and statism were each pressing against a rubber ball.
When individualism presses hard in the direction
of anarchy, it is checked by the counteracting
forces of the state and the groups. The development of individuals through education and other
techniques does not mean that the country is
headed for anarchy. The fact that farmers form
co-operative associations for group action does not
mean that the country is headed for syndicalism.
Increases in the services of government to farmers
as individuals, to farmers as groups, or to farmers
as a whole, does not mean that the country is
headed for state socialism.

This elastic balance, this democratic give-and-
take, is best maintained when there is movement
between the three categories, when citizens who

operate farms are also active in farm organizations and in government services. The colleges of agriculture will do well if their future graduates are young men and women who have an understanding of the framework of science, and of the needs of man and of the world in which man lives; who are familiar with the technique of good farming; who have studied political science, cultural anthropology, psychology and economics as they apply to agriculture; who, above all, have a philosophy and a religion of life. When these people establish themselves on the soil as working farmers, working family farmers, their philosophy of life will lead them to interest in their local government and their co-operative association, in the formation of national policies, in the national government. They can start up the ladder of election, acquiring a basis of local experience on school boards, boards of county commissioners, boards of directors of county farm organizations. In the give-and-take of policy formation for these institutions they will function as leaders of little discussion groups in their neighborhoods. Administrative experience will come through membership on county farm security committees, advising and helping with the making of rehabilitation loans and farm tenant purchases, through membership on county agricultural planning boards, boards of directors of soil conservation districts, and county and community committees of the Agricultural Adjustment Administration. With the technique and the quality of persuasiveness which comes only from participation and experience, they will develop local agricultural democracies.

Members of this democratic type of society will gradually be sent by fellow members as representatives on state agricultural administrative institutions, state planning boards, state Agricultural Adjustment Administration committees, or to become state legislators, where they will learn to deal with problems of the towns and cities as well as the farms. Later they will be asked to accept positions of leadership and responsibility in connection with national agricultural affairs, serving both agriculture and the general welfare as members of the national legislative bodies, or as administrators in the Department of Agriculture, or as officers in the national co-operative and farm organizations.

This process, if it could go on for a generation, would form a link that would tie the old, highly respected, agricultural democracy of Jefferson to the new, functioning, agricultural democracy of the future. The signs of the times point toward a new great surge of agricultural democracy in which there is both over-all unity and place for different viewpoints, different programs, different patterns, different political parties, with reference to details. It behooves all who believe in this promise to put their shoulders to the wheel and with tolerance and good nature push along to make the new agricultural democracy a reality.